THE
SOLAR
SYSTEM

This edition published by Scholastic Inc.,
557 Broadway, New York, NY 10012
by arrangement with Quarto publishing.

Distributed by
Scholastic Canada Ltd., Markham, Ontario

Copyright © QEB Publishing 2008

Published in the United States by
QEB Publishing, Inc.
3 Wrigley, Suite A
Irvine, CA 92618
www.qeb-publishing.com

Library of Congress Control Numbers:
2008012590, 2008012583, 2008012589, 2008012595,
2008012588, 2008012587

ISBN: 978-1-59566-135-7
Print Line: 11 10 9 8 7 6 5 4 3 2

Printed in Toppan Leefung Printing Ltd, China

Author Rosalind Mist
Consultant Terry Jennings
Editor Amanda Askew
Designer Melissa Alaverdy
Picture Researcher Maria Joannou
Illustrator Richard Burgess

Words in **bold**
can be found
in the glossary
on P.118.

THE
SOLAR
SYSTEM

Rosalind Mist

QEB Publishing

Contents

Asteroids, Comets, and Meteors

The Solar System

The Solar System is made up of the Sun and everything that orbits, **or circles, it.** This includes the planets and their moons, as well as **meteors, asteroids,** and **comets.**

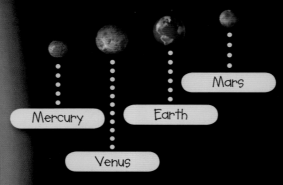

Mercury

Venus

Earth

Mars

Jupiter

The Sun is at the center of our solar system. It is 100 million miles (161 million km) from Earth.

Sun

STAR FACT!
We can see some planets shining in the night sky because they reflect light from the Sun.

The sizes of the planets are roughly to scale, but the distances between them are not to scale.

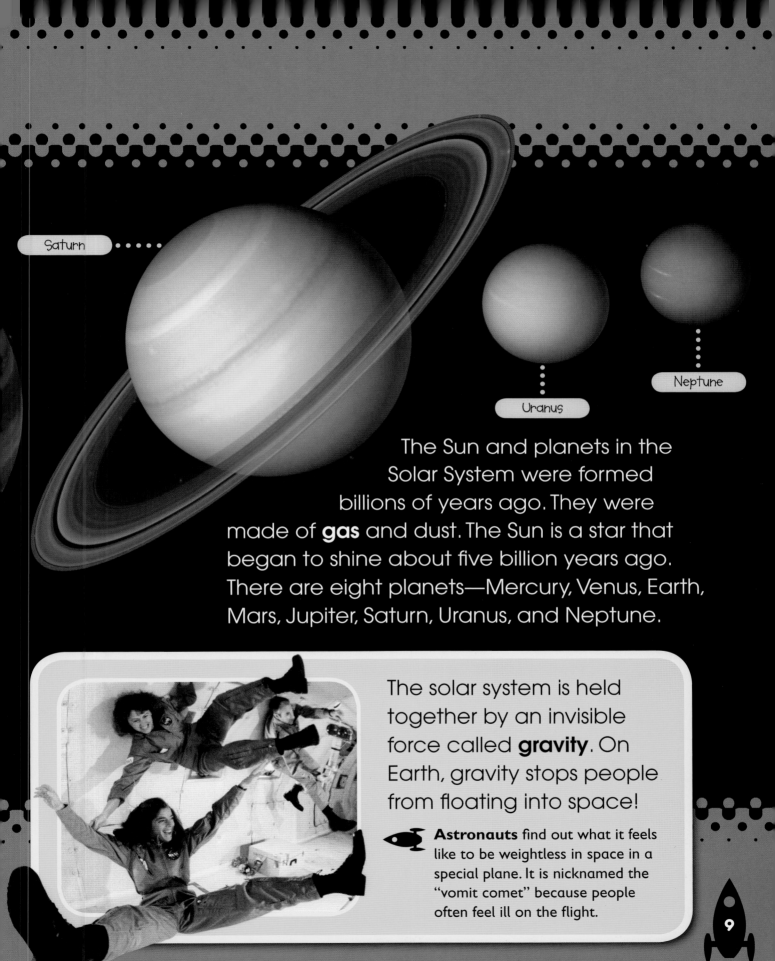

Saturn

Uranus

Neptune

The Sun and planets in the Solar System were formed billions of years ago. They were made of **gas** and dust. The Sun is a star that began to shine about five billion years ago. There are eight planets—Mercury, Venus, Earth, Mars, Jupiter, Saturn, Uranus, and Neptune.

The solar system is held together by an invisible force called **gravity**. On Earth, gravity stops people from floating into space!

Astronauts find out what it feels like to be weightless in space in a special plane. It is nicknamed the "vomit comet" because people often feel ill on the flight.

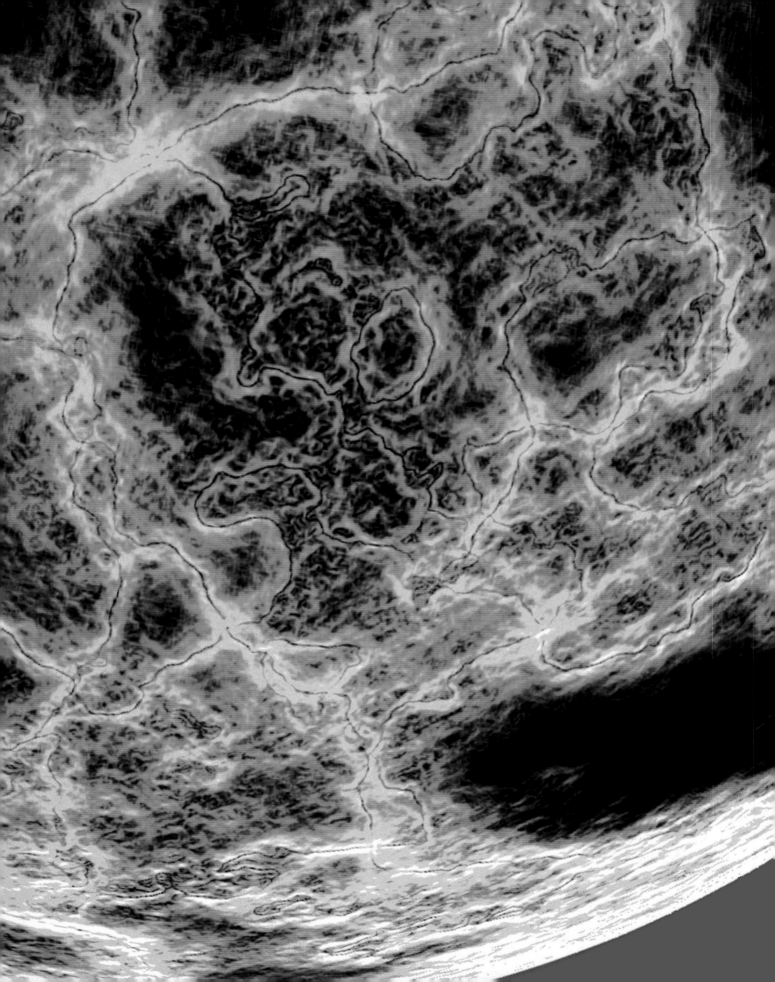

SUN
AND
MOON

The Sun

The Sun is a star, just like the stars that you can see in the sky at night. It is at the center of our solar system and is the nearest star to the Earth.

The Sun is not solid like Earth, but is a huge ball of very hot, burning gas. It sends out heat and light into space.

STAR FACT!
The Sun looks larger than other stars because it is nearer to the Earth. The next star is nearly 300,000 times further away.

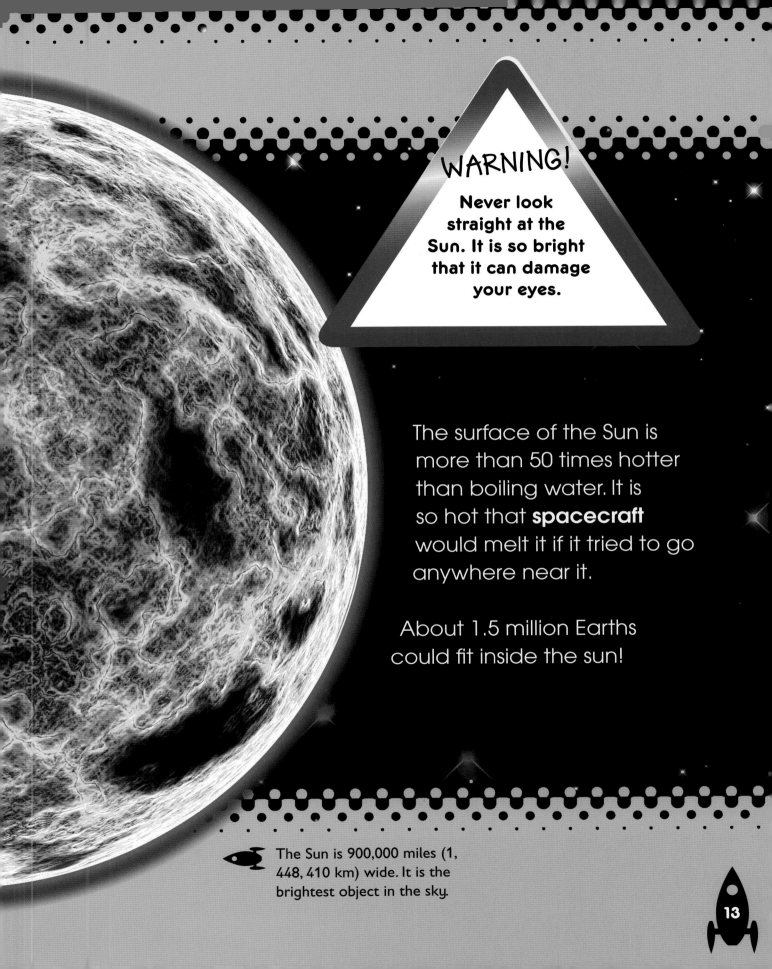

The surface of the Sun is more than 50 times hotter than boiling water. It is so hot that **spacecraft** would melt it if it tried to go anywhere near it.

About 1.5 million Earths could fit inside the sun!

The Sun is 900,000 miles (1, 448, 410 km) wide. It is the brightest object in the sky.

Sunlight

The Sun produces light, which travels 100 million miles (161 million km) to the Earth. It only takes eight minutes and 20 seconds for the Sun's rays to reach the Earth.

We can only see things when there is light. At nighttime, without any sunlight, it is dark and colder than in the daytime.

 When one side of the Earth faces the Sun, it is daytime. On the opposite side of the Earth, where there is no sunlight, it is nighttime.

Nighttime

Daytime

Sunlight is made of many different colors, not just yellow. There are seven colors—red, orange, yellow, green, blue, indigo, and violet. When sunlight passes through raindrops, a rainbow forms and all the colors can be seen.

Without the Sun, plants would not grow. Animals, including humans, need plants to eat.

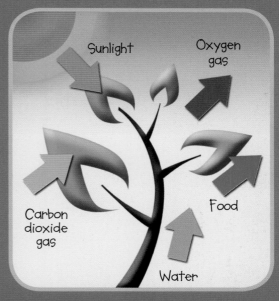

Sunlight

Oxygen gas

Carbon dioxide gas

Food

Water

🚀 Plants use sunlight to turn **carbon dioxide** gas and water into food and **oxygen** gas.

🚀 A rainbow makes a curve across the sky. The outside edge of a rainbow is red and the inside edge is violet.

Make your own rainbow

· · · · · · · · · · · · · ·

Stand next to a wall and shine a flashlight on an old CD. Move the CD around. Can you see a rainbow on the wall? Can you see the seven different colors?

Stormy Sun

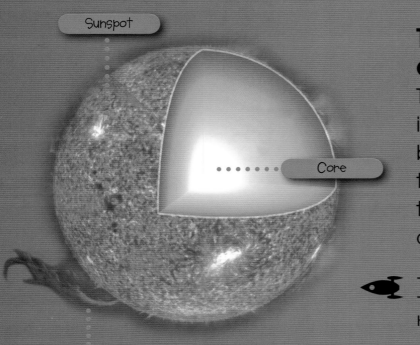

Sunspot

Core

Flames of gas

The Sun produces heat as well as light.

The core, or middle, of the Sun is the hottest part. Hot gases bubble up from the core to the surface of the Sun. When the gases burn, heat and light are produced.

The Sun is made of many layers. The core is nearly 3,000 times hotter than the surface.

The surface of the Sun has dark areas called sunspots. They are cooler than the hot, yellow areas.

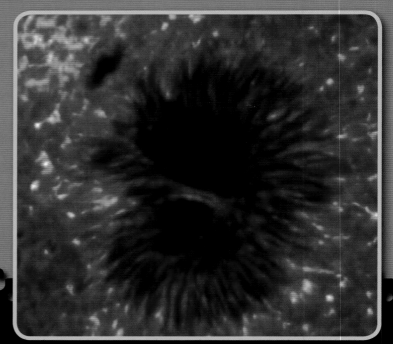

Sunspots were discovered by the **astronomer** Galileo Galilei. Some sunspots can last for

The Sun throws huge loops of hot gas into space. These flames are enormous explosions—even bigger than the Earth!

 As the gases on the Sun burn, they create huge fiery storms. This flame of gas is about 190,000 miles (305, 775 km) across —that is more than 23 Earths!

Flame of gas

STAR FACT!
We can use the Sun's energy. Some **solar panels** soak up the Sun's heat to warm water. Others soak up light and then change it into electricity.

Solar eclipse

When the Moon moves directly between the Sun and the Earth, there is a solar eclipse. This is because the Moon blocks the Sun, stopping sunlight from reaching the Earth. Everywhere becomes dark, just like nighttime. Sometimes the Moon covers the whole Sun, and sometimes only part of it.

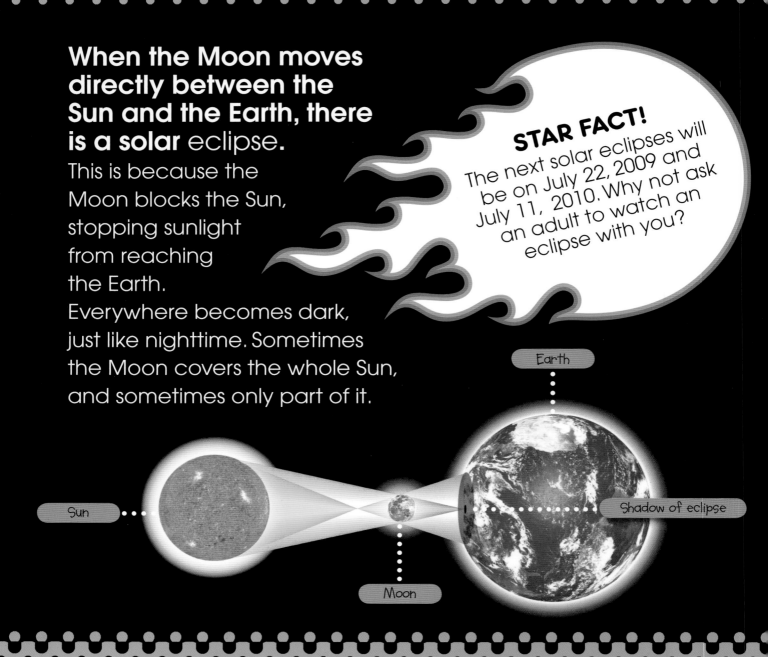

Earth

Sun

Moon

Shadow of eclipse

 When the Moon completely blocks the Sun, it is called a total eclipse.

Special solar eclipse glasses block out the dangerous rays of sunlight to protect your eyes.

People need to wear special glasses when looking at an eclipse; otherwise, their eyes could be damaged. Scientists can see hot gas around the Sun during an eclipse. The gas stretches for 650,000 miles (1,046,074 km) into space.

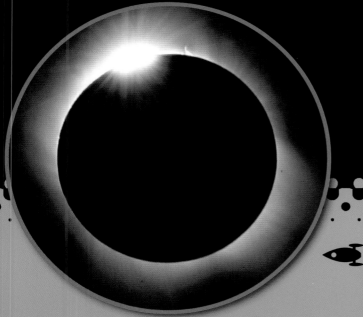

The hot gas around the Sun, called the **corona,** normally cannot be seen.

When the Moon first starts to move away, the Sun's corona looks like a sparkling diamond ring.

The Moon

The Moon is a round, hard, rocky ball.

It is smaller than the Earth—in fact, nearly four Moons could fit across the Earth. The Moon orbits, or circles, the Earth.

Earth

The Moon is the brightest object in the night sky.

Moon

The Moon is made of pale-colored rocks. These rocks reflect the light from the Sun. The Moon does not make its own light.

The Sun and Moon seem to be about the same size from Earth, but the Sun is really much bigger than the Moon. They only seem to be the same size because the Sun is a lot further away than the Moon.

We always see the same side of the Moon. By sending rockets into space, we can see what the other side of the Moon looks like. There are more craters and fewer dark areas.

Largest crater

The largest crater in our solar system is on the far side of the Moon. It is 1,500 miles (2,414 km) across—about half as big as the U.S.

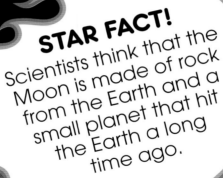

STAR FACT!
Scientists think that the Moon is made of rock from the Earth and a small planet that hit the Earth a long time ago.

On the surface

When rocks crash into the Moon, they make holes called craters.
Some craters are so wide that a large city, such as London, England, could fit inside! There are about 500,000 craters that are larger than 0.5 miles (0.8 km)—that is as long as 20 Olympic swimming pools.

Plain

STAR FACT!
You can see the Moon in the daytime as well as at night, but it is often more difficult to find.

The Moon also has many dark and light areas. The dark areas are called **plains**. They are flat and filled with rock made from **lava**. The light areas are higher than the plains.

 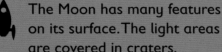 The Moon has many features on its surface. The light areas are covered in craters.

Moon gazing

Go outside at night with an adult and look at the Moon. Use a pair of binoculars or a telescope if possible. Can you see the dark areas? Can you see the craters?

Rock and dust around the edge of a crater blasted out when the crater was made.

Full Moon, Half Moon

It takes about one month for the Moon to go around the Earth once.

The Moon seems to change shape because as it moves, different parts are in sunlight. We see the parts that reflect sunlight. The rest of the Moon is in shadow and we cannot see it.

Full Moon

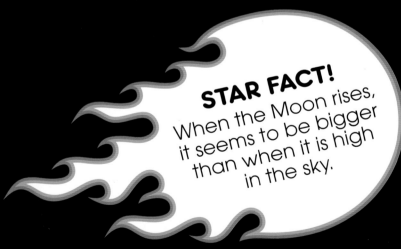

STAR FACT!
When the Moon rises, it seems to be bigger than when it is high in the sky.

The changing shapes of the bright part of the Moon are called the phases of the Moon.

When the Moon looks round, it is called a Full Moon. When only part of the Moon can be seen, it is called a Half Moon.

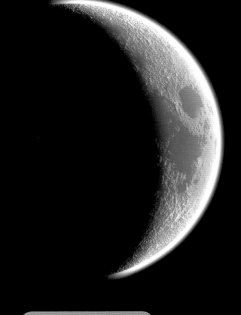

Half Moon

Crescent Moon

A Crescent Moon looks like a big bite has been taken out of it! When there is a New Moon, it is in complete shadow and we cannot see the Moon at all.

Moon study

. . . .

For a month, draw what the Moon looks like each night. Can you label the different phases of the Moon? Can you explain why the Moon changes shape?

Flying to the Moon

It is a long way to the Moon —about 240,000 miles (386,243 km).
If you could drive a car to the Moon, it would take more than four months to get there! Astronauts are people who go into space. They travel in rockets and shuttles, which move very

STAR FACT!
On Earth, we see the Moon rise and set. Astronauts who orbit the Moon see the Earth rise and set instead!

In the 1960s and 1970s, astronauts traveled to the Moon in the Apollo spacecraft. It only took three days to get there.

 The most famous mission to the Moon was the Apollo 11 mission in 1969

Today, astronauts go into space in the **space shuttle**. The shuttle goes to the **International Space Station**, not the Moon.

Astronauts used lunar **rovers** to travel around the Moon. They brought some Moon rocks back to Earth. Scientists used them to find out how old the Moon is.

When astronauts drove around the Moon, they found it was rocky, dusty, and dry.

Scientists also send **space probes** to the Moon. They carry experiments to tell scientists what the Moon is made of. So far, the probes have found cooled lava, metals, and even ice!

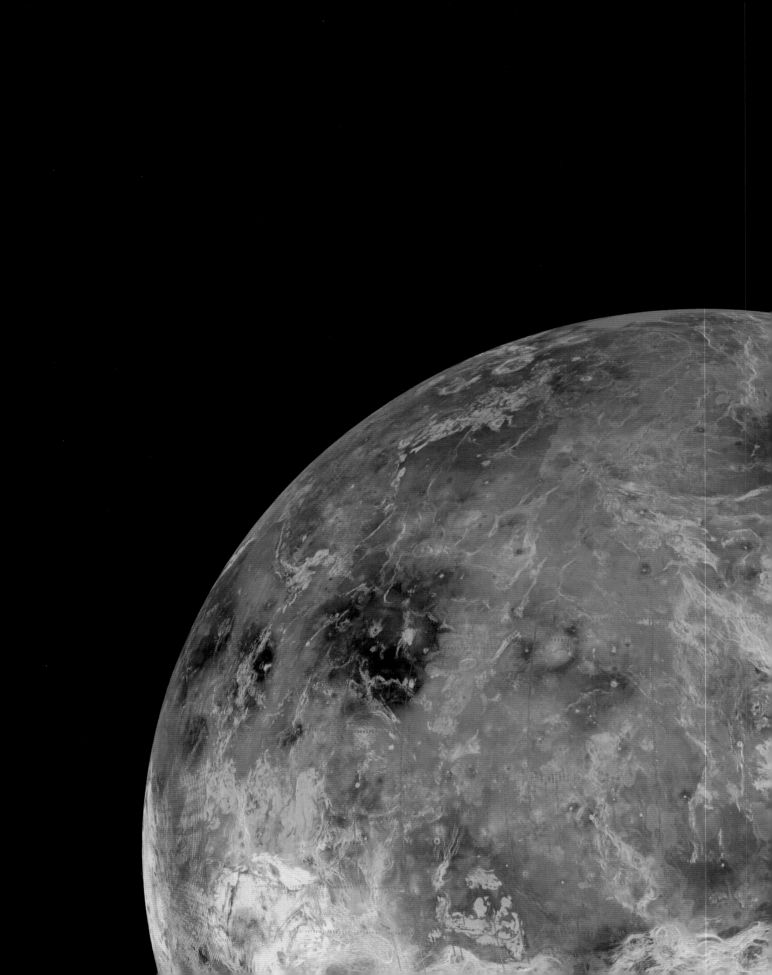

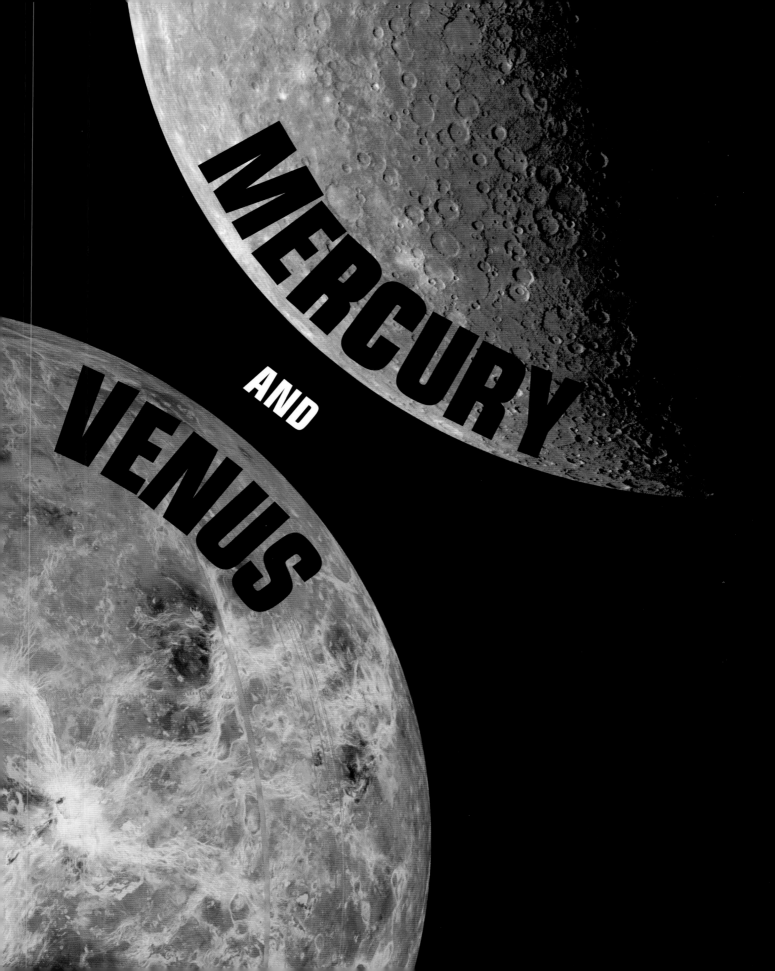

MERCURY AND VENUS

Mercury

Mercury is the closest planet to the Sun.
It is also the smallest planet in our solar system, slightly bigger than Earth's Moon. Mercury does not have a moon of its own.

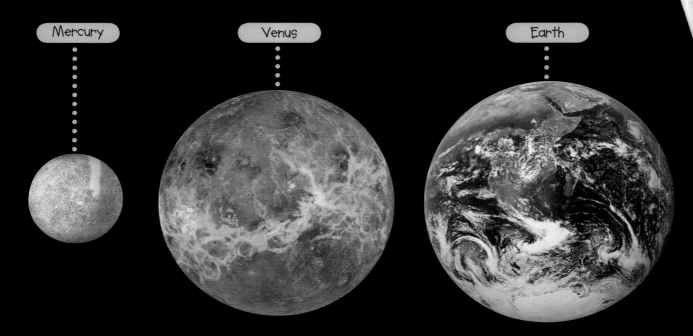

Mercury   Venus   Earth

Mercury is a dry, rocky planet. Its surface is covered in holes called **craters**. The craters were made when meteors and comets crashed into the planet.

 Mercury and Venus are both hard, rocky planets, but they are very different from each other.

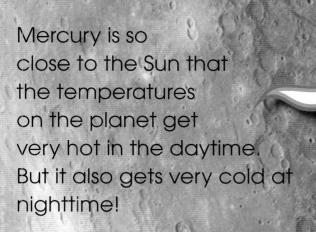

Mercury is so close to the Sun that the temperatures on the planet get very hot in the daytime. But it also gets very cold at nighttime!

 Mercury looks like the Moon. The craters are billions of years old. They were made when our solar system formed.

Hot and cold

Mercury is unusual because it spins so slowly.
A day on Mercury is 176 Earth days. Mercury travels around the Sun once every 88 days, so a year on Mercury is only 88 Earth days—the day is twice as long as the year!

 On Mercury, there is daylight for 88 days and then darkness for 88 days.

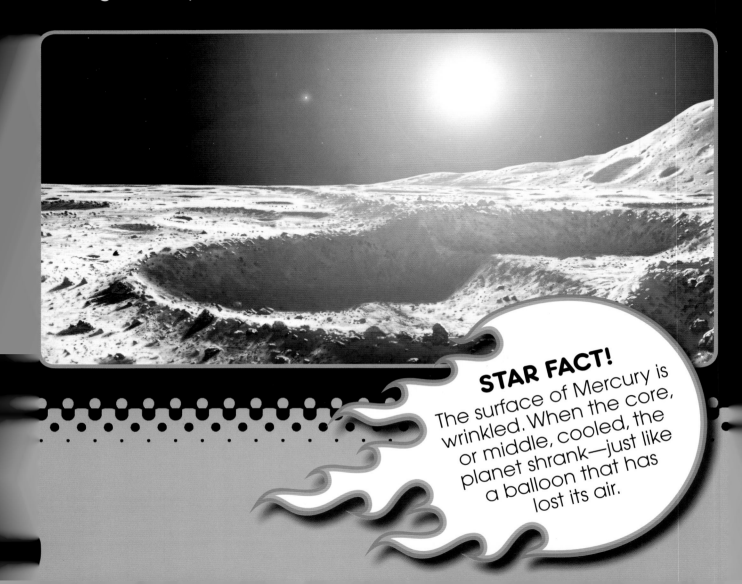

STAR FACT!
The surface of Mercury is wrinkled. When the core, or middle, cooled, the planet shrank—just like a balloon that has lost its air.

Mercury gets very hot during the 88 days of sunlight. The temperature can reach 800°F(427°C), so hot that it could melt **lead**.

The dark side of Mercury is so dark that nothing can be seen. In 2008, scientists saw a complete close-up of Mercury for the first time, including the dark side.

When the Sun sets, Mercury cools down to -290°F (-179°C). If Earth were ever to get that cold, the air would start to turn from gas into liquid.

A cratered world

Mercury is almost completely covered in craters.

Some of the deep craters near Mercury's north pole never get any sunlight. Scientists think that they might have found ice in these craters, even though Mercury is so close to the Sun.

The biggest crater is Caloris Basin. It is 960 miles (1,545 km) across and one mile (1.6 km) deep.

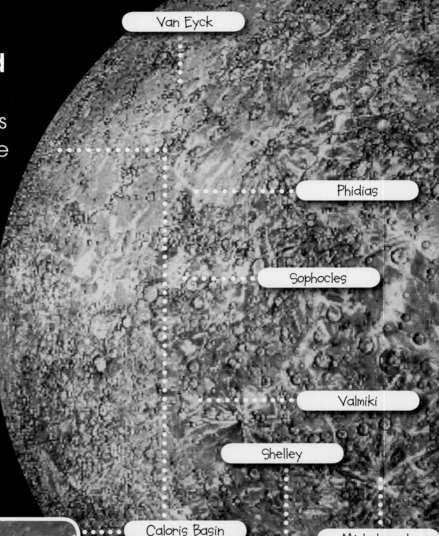

Van Eyck

Phidias

Sophocles

Valmiki

Shelley

Caloris Basin

Michelangelo

Wagner

Bach

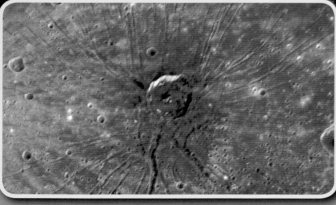

The "spider" crater inside Caloris Basin has lots of grooves that look like spiders' legs.

Spacecraft have taken pictures of Mercury's wrinkled, cratered surface.

Vivaldi

Renoir

Chekhov

Schubert

Many of the craters were made when the planet was hit by an asteroid or comet, but some were made by **volcanoes**. **Space probes** have also taken pictures of smooth areas called **plains**, similar to the "seas" on the Moon.

Smooth plains

Melting ice

Find out if ice melts more quickly in sunlight or in shade. Take two ice cubes out of the freezer. Put one on a plate in the sunlight. Put one on a plate in the shade. Which one melts first?

Mercury's plains can be smooth and flat, or filled with craters.

Exploring the planets

To explore the planets, scientists often use space probes.
Space probes can either fly past or orbit a planet. Some space probes land on the surface of the rocky planets or moons.

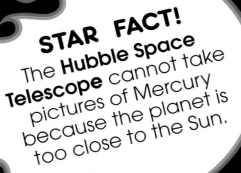

STAR FACT!
The **Hubble Space Telescope** cannot take pictures of Mercury because the planet is too close to the Sun.

 Mercury Messenger was launched in 2004. It will pass Mercury three times before it can start orbiting the planet in 2011.

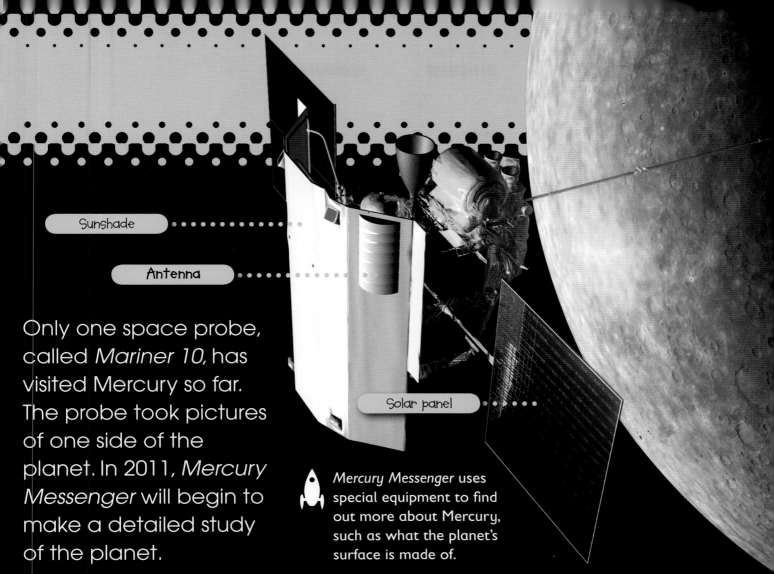

Sunshade

Antenna

Solar panel

Only one space probe, called *Mariner 10*, has visited Mercury so far. The probe took pictures of one side of the planet. In 2011, *Mercury Messenger* will begin to make a detailed study of the planet.

Mercury Messenger uses special equipment to find out more about Mercury, such as what the planet's surface is made of.

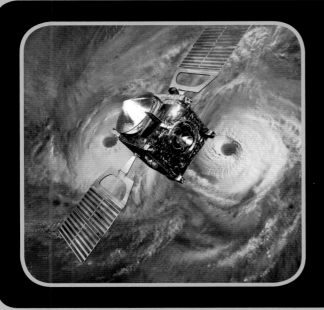

Venus has been visited by 20 space probes and is the most visited planet in the solar system. *Venus Express* is there now. It is looking at Venus' clouds and surface.

Venus Express reached Venus in 2006. Its wings are **solar panels** that collect sunlight to provide power for the spacecraft.

Venus

Venus is the second planet from the Sun.

It orbits the Sun between Mercury and Earth. Venus is about the same size as Earth, but looks very different. Like Mercury, it is a planet without a moon.

Venus was the first planet ever to be visited and landed on by a space probe. The surface of Venus is very smooth—it does not have many craters.

Finding Venus

You can see Venus either in the evening or in the morning.

The Evening Star
Venus is the first bright light you see after the Sun sets.

The Morning Star
Venus is the last bright light you see before the Sun rises.

Pictures have been made of Venus to show what it would look like if it had no clouds.

The clouds around Venus are so thick that scientists use special instruments to see the surface.

Venus can be seen in the sky if it is not too close to the Sun. It looks like a very bright star that does not twinkle.

Moon

Venus

 After the Sun and the Moon, Venus is the brightest object in the sky. It is so bright that it can sometimes be seen when there are no stars in the sky.

Hot, hot, hot

A planet warms up when it is in sunlight.

The closer a planet is to the Sun, the warmer the sunlight is. Mercury should be the hottest planet, but Venus gets hotter than Mercury, even though Venus is farther from the Sun!

 Mercury has almost no atmosphere because wind from the Sun sweeps it all away.

Venus becomes hot because it has a very thick **atmosphere**. An atmosphere is a layer of gases surrounding a planet or a moon—it stops heat from escaping. Venus' atmosphere is much thicker than the Earth's. It is mostly made of a gas called **carbon dioxide**.

 It is always cloudy on Venus! The clouds on Venus are not made of water— they are made of acid.

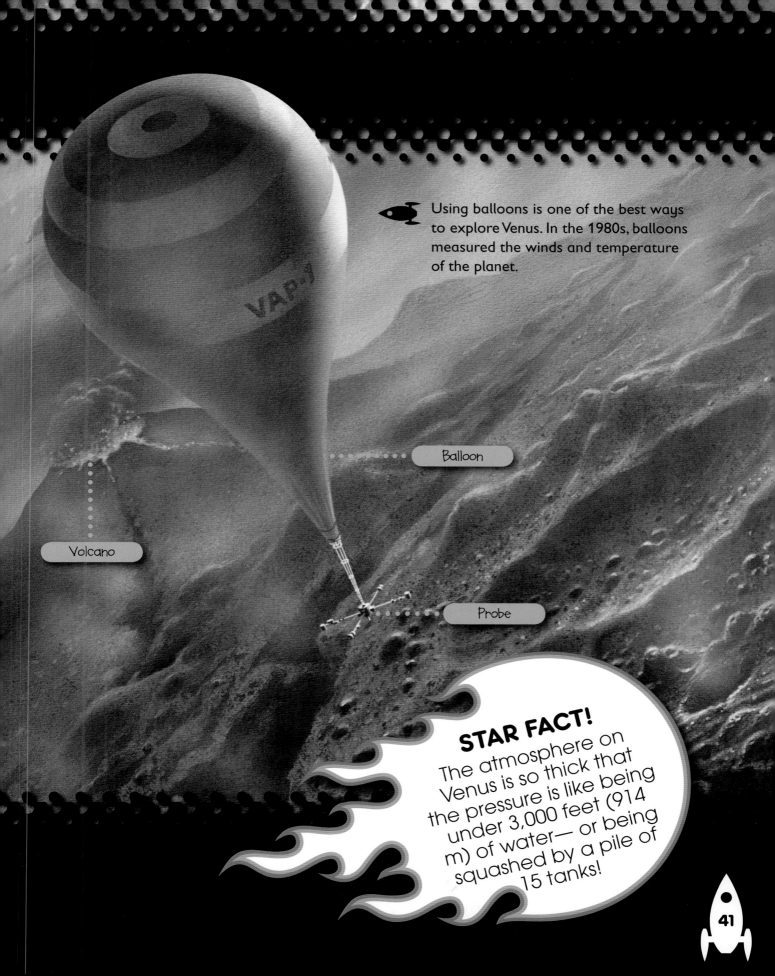

Using balloons is one of the best ways to explore Venus. In the 1980s, balloons measured the winds and temperature of the planet.

VAP-1

Balloon

Volcano

Probe

STAR FACT!
The atmosphere on Venus is so thick that the pressure is like being under 3,000 feet (914 m) of water— or being squashed by a pile of 15 tanks!

Crossing the Sun

Sometimes Venus passes between the Sun and Earth.
This is called a **transit** and can actually be seen from Earth. The planet appears as a small dot crossing the face of the Sun!

 Transits occur when a planet moves directly between the Sun and Earth. Only Mercury and Venus can transit the Sun.

STAR FACT!
Mercury transits happen quite often—about 13 times in 100 years. The last transit took place on November 8, 2006.

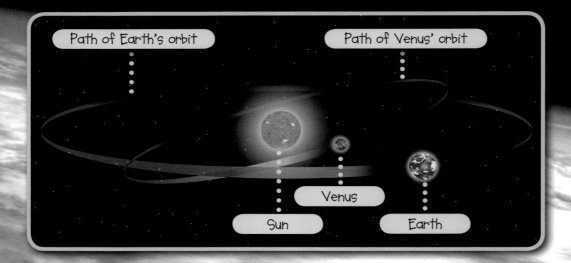

Path of Earth's orbit

Path of Venus' orbit

Earth

Venus

Sun

Earth

Sun

Venus

The planet blocks out a circle of sunlight, so it looks like a black dot on the face of the Sun.

Transits of Venus only take place every few hundred years—and then two happen within eight years! Scientists can now predict when transits will appear.

You must use special glasses to look at the Sun. They block out all the dangerous rays.

The last transit of Venus was on June 8, 2004—it lasted for six hours. The next transit will be on June 5 to 6, 2012.

Volcanoes

Venus is so cloudy, we cannot see the surface.
However, scientists discovered that underneath the clouds, Venus has many volcanoes.

 Hot, runny rock called **magma** came up from volcanoes on Venus. It came to the surface as **lava** cooled to give Venus a smooth surface.

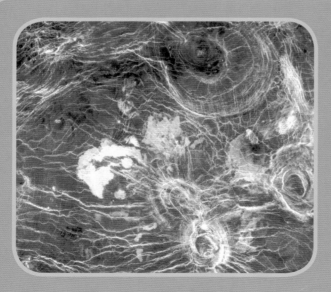

Venus has more volcanoes than any other planet in our solar system—more than 1,600 major volcanoes have been discovered. Most of the volcanoes on Venus are probably **inactive**.

 On Venus, the unusual "spider" shapes are large volcanic holes surrounded by many cracks.

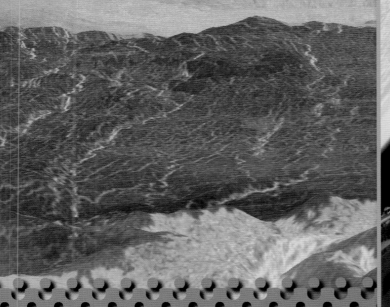

STAR FACT!
Venus has many large volcanoes and thousands of smaller ones. It also has other unusual volcanic features not found on Earth.

The biggest volcano on Venus is Maat Mons. It is 5 miles (8 km) in height—almost as tall as Mount Everest. The *Magellan* probe has seen signs that may mean Maat Mons is still active.

 The *Magellan* probe spent more than four years orbiting Venus to create a map of the planet's surface.

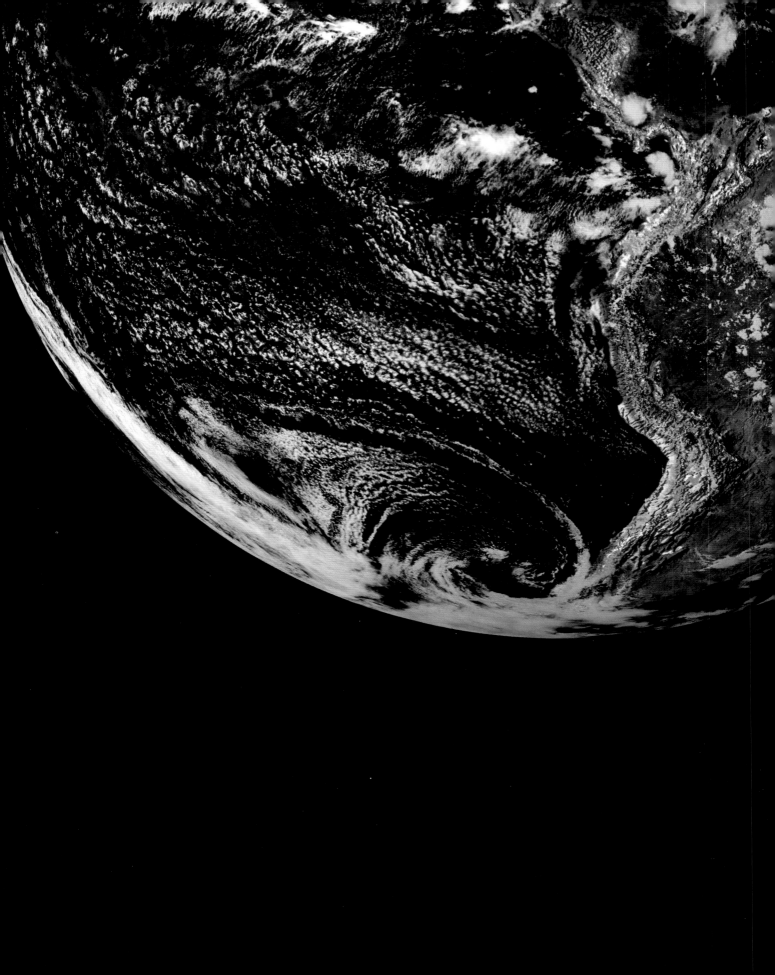

EARTH AND MARS

Planet Earth

Earth is the planet we live on.

It is the third planet from the Sun, between Mars and Venus. From space, it looks like a blue, green, and white marble. This is because it is covered with oceans, land, and clouds. In fact, 70 percent of the Earth's surface is covered by water!

STAR FACT!
The Earth formed about 4,600 million years ago. It started as huge clouds of swirling gas and dust.

Moon

Earth

Earth also has a moon. It is dry and dusty, has no air, and is covered in **craters**.

Although Earth is large, its atmosphere is very thin.

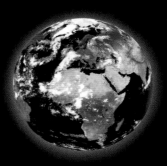

A thin layer of air surrounds Earth. This is called the **atmosphere**. It lets plants and animals, including humans, breathe. This makes Earth special because it is the only planet so far where life is possible.

Satellites take pictures of Earth from space. Scientists use these to study the weather and find out about Earth's land and seas.

Inside the Earth

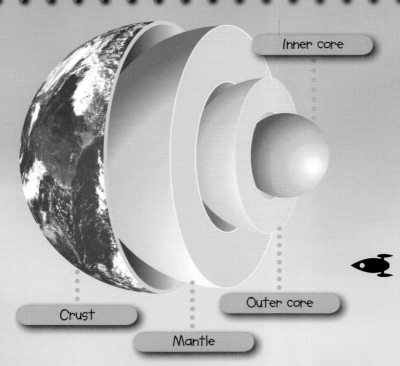

Inner core

Crust

Mantle

Outer core

The Earth is made up of four different layers.

The crust is the layer that we live on. It is made of giant slabs of solid rock that float on hot, soft rock underneath.

The Earth is like an onion, with four layers. To find out about the layers, scientists measure how earthquakes travel through the Earth.

Below the crust is a layer of hot rock called the mantle. In places, the rock is so hot that it has melted. This molten rock is called **magma**. When a **volcano** erupts, the magma bursts out. Then it is called **lava**.

STAR FACT!

Where parts of Earth's crust bump into each other, mountains are pushed up, volcanoes erupt, and earthquakes take place.

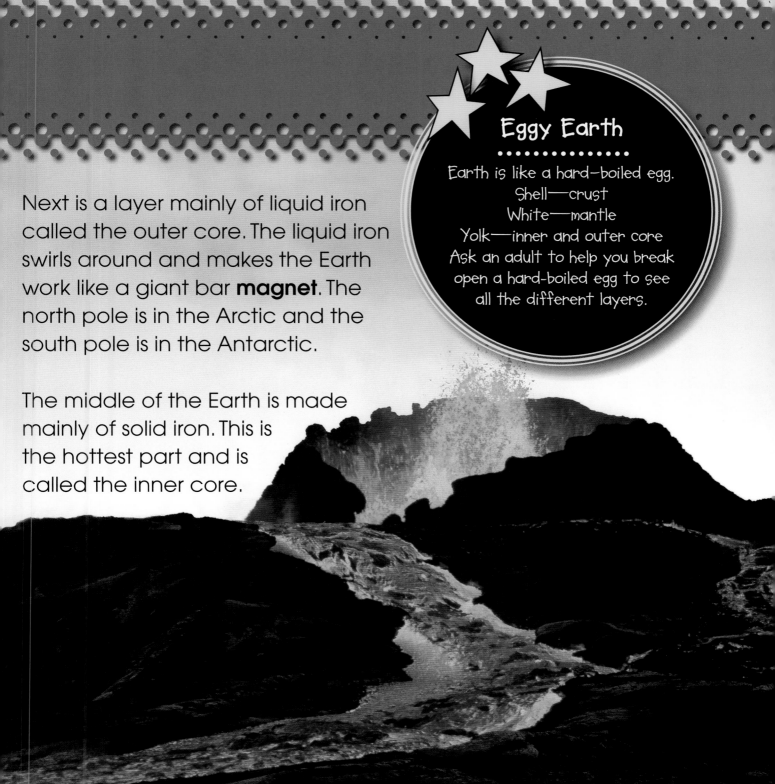

Next is a layer mainly of liquid iron called the outer core. The liquid iron swirls around and makes the Earth work like a giant bar **magnet**. The north pole is in the Arctic and the south pole is in the Antarctic.

The middle of the Earth is made mainly of solid iron. This is the hottest part and is called the inner core.

Eggy Earth

· · · · · · · · · · · · · · ·

Earth is like a hard—boiled egg.
Shell—crust
White—mantle
Yolk—inner and outer core
Ask an adult to help you break open a hard-boiled egg to see all the different layers.

 The magma, or molten rock, inside the Earth is very hot and soft. It can flow out of volcanoes in red-hot rivers of lava.

Day and night

The Earth spins around like a spinning top.

It turns all the way around in 24 hours a day. In a day, the whole world, except for the poles, will have daytime and nighttime. Only one side of the Earth faces the Sun at any one time. Sunlight shines on this side and it is daytime. On the side that is not facing the Sun, it is nighttime.

Daytime in South America

As the Earth spins, the Sun shines on one half of the Earth, and it is daytime.

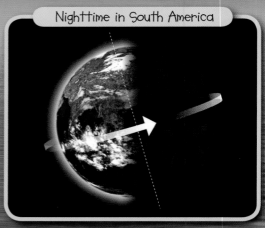

Nighttime in South America

When the same side turns away from the Sun, it goes dark, and daytime turns into nighttime.

Shadows

Stand outside on a sunny day and look at the ground. Can you see your shadow? Make different shadows using a flashlight and a piece of paper —it works best in a dark room.

 At sunset and sunrise, the sky can turn red and orange, or even pink.

When the Sun seems to go down, or sets, your part of the Earth is turning away from it. This time of day is called dusk. When the Sun seems to come up, or rises, the part of the Earth that you are on is turning toward it. This is called dawn.

During summer, in the northern part of the world, the Sun never sets completely. It is light for 24 hours a day. This is called the midnight Sun.

 During the day, the Sun rises and falls, making a path across the sky.

The seasons

The Earth orbits, or circles, the Sun.
It takes a year to go around the Sun once.
In this year, we have four seasons—spring,
summer, fall, and winter.

The Earth's **axis** is tilted. As the Earth
moves around the Sun during the year,
the amount of sunlight in different parts
changes. When northern areas, such as
Europe and North America, are tilted
toward the Sun, it is summer, but
when they are tilted
away, it is winter.

 The seasons occur
because the Earth's
axis is tilted. When
one part of the Earth
points toward the Sun,
it is summer. When the
same part points away,
it is winter.

STAR FACT!
Seasons in Australia are
the opposite of those in
Europe. When Europe
is tilted toward the Sun,
Australia is tilted away,
and vice versa!

Summer

 In summer, the days are long and the
Sun is high in the sky. The weather is
warm and flowers are fully grown.

In spring, the Sun gets higher in the sky and the days become longer. Plants start to grow and baby animals are born.

Spring

In winter, the Sun is low and the days are short. The weather is cold and many plants die.

Winter

In fall, the days begin to shorten and the Sun is lower. It is cooler and trees lose their leaves.

Fall

Mars, the red planet

Mars is the fourth planet from the Sun, between Earth and Jupiter.
It is about half the size of Earth. The planet is red-orange in color because it has rusty-red soil.

Mars

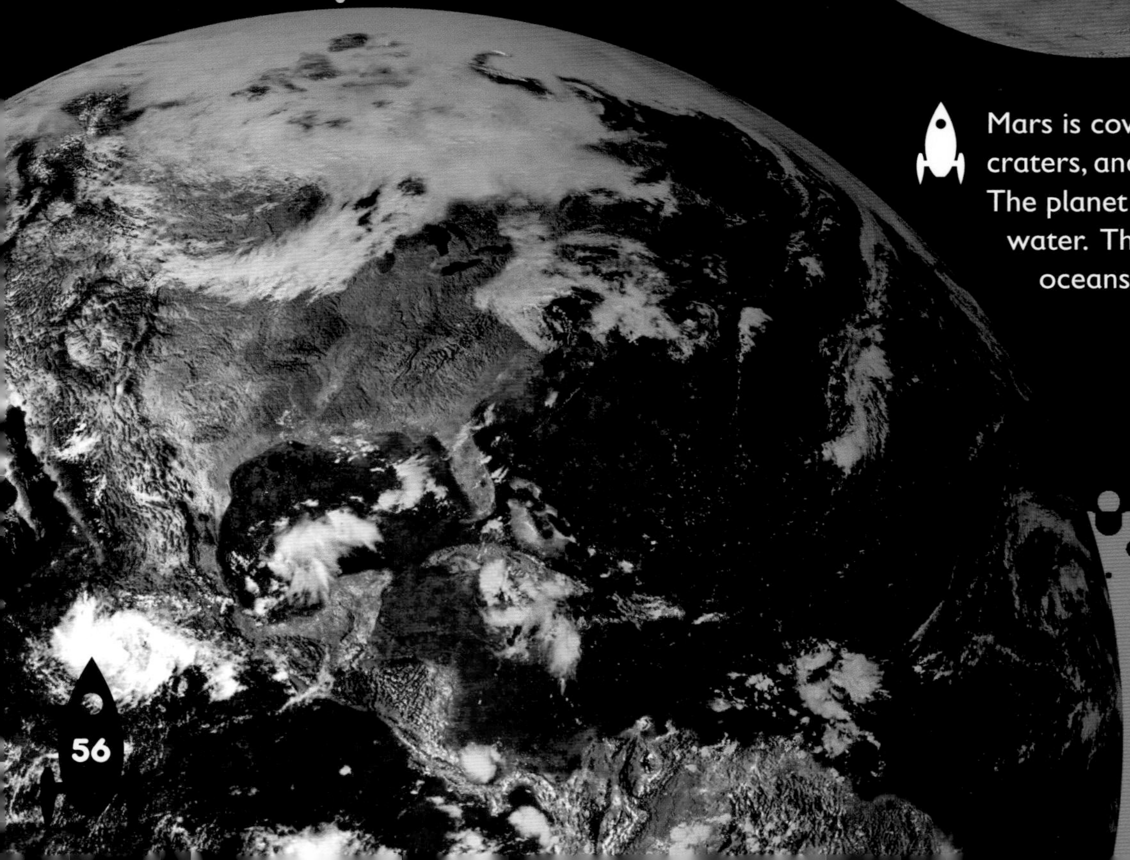

Earth

Mars is covered in hills, craters, and volcanoes. The planet has no liquid water. There are no oceans or lakes.

Mars has a dry, rocky surface. Scientists think that Mars used to have liquid water, but now the only water that has been found is in the polar **ice caps**.

Phobos

Deimos

The surface of Mars looks like a dry, rocky desert. The Mars Exploration Rovers have to find their way around the rocks as they explore Mars.

Phobos and Deimos look like asteroids. They may have come from the Asteroid Belt.

Mars has two moons called Phobos and Deimos. They are chunks of rock, much smaller than our Moon. They are covered in craters. Phobos speeds around Mars once every 7.5 hours. Deimos takes 30 hours to orbit, or circle, Mars.

STAR FACT!
Sometimes Mars has a pink sunset because of the red dust in the air.

On Mars

Mars has a volcano called Olympus Mons—the largest and highest volcano in our solar system. It is about three times as tall as Mount Everest, the tallest mountain on Earth.

STAR FACT!
Olympus Mons covers almost the same area as the UK.

Victoria crater

Olympus Mons

Valles Marineris

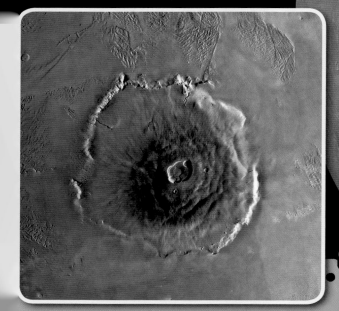

 Olympus Mons has not erupted for at least two million years.

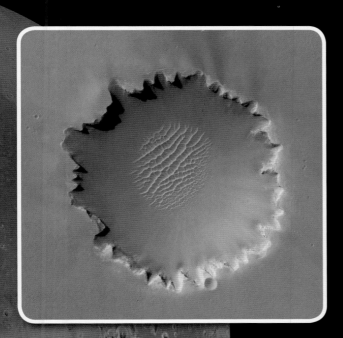

 The Victoria crater is about 2,400 feet (732 m) across. The Mars Exploration Rover, *Opportunity*, is exploring it.

When a large rock crashes onto a planet or moon, it leaves a big crater. Mars is covered in lots of craters.

Valles Marineris is the biggest canyon in our solar system. It goes nearly a quarter of the way around Mars!

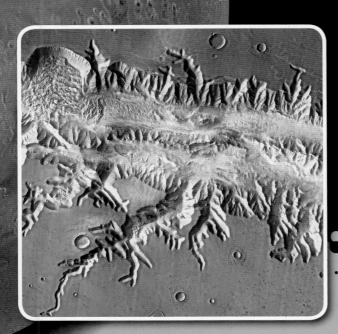

 Valles Marineris is enormous, at more than 1,800 miles (2,897 km) in length. The Grand Canyon in the U.S. would fit into just a small part of it!

Stormy planet

On Mars, there can be very fast winds.

Sometimes the whole planet is one big dust storm!

STAR FACT!
On Mars, there is very little water, but sometimes there are thin clouds. It never rains on Mars.

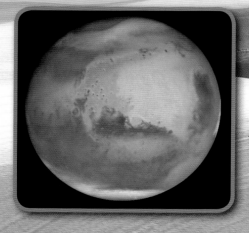

 The red areas are dust from volcanoes and the dark areas are rock. The dust is blown around by the wind in huge dust storms.

Mars has dust devils, which are swirls of wind and dust—like mini tornadoes. The robotic rovers that are exploring Mars get very dusty. Every time the swirling winds of a dust devil go by, the rovers get cleaned.

 Dust devils on Mars can be small and gentle, but they can also be much bigger than those on Earth.

A long, deep valley near Mars' north pole. The light and dark areas show layers of ice and sand.

Christiaan Huygens (1629–1695)

Christiaan Huygens was the first person to see a white spot on Mars. We now know that this is an ice cap. Huygens also found out that a day on Mars is nearly as long as a day on Earth.

Ice cap

Mars has ice caps, just like Earth. By watching the ice caps on Mars, scientists figured out that Mars has seasons, too. In summer, the ice melts and the ice caps get smaller. In winter, the ice caps grow again.

Exploring Mars

Many space probes have visited Mars. Some have even landed on the surface.

In 2004, two Mars Exploration Rovers, *Spirit* and *Opportunity*, landed on Mars. They are like large remote-controlled cars. Scientists on Earth drive them slowly over the planet. They have climbed hills and explored craters.

Camera

Antenna to send information back to Earth

Tool to collect rocks

 Spirit moves slowly to make sure it does not get stuck or miss anything interesting.

The rovers can take photos of Mars. They can also measure how hot it is there. They have special tools to test the different rocks and can even collect dust from the air.

The rovers have made many discoveries. Scientists now think that there may have been liquid water on Mars a long time ago.

By looking at what types of rock there are on Mars, scientists can figure out what Mars used to be like.

STAR FACT!
The Mars Exploration Rovers were only meant to work for three months, but they are still working after more than four years.

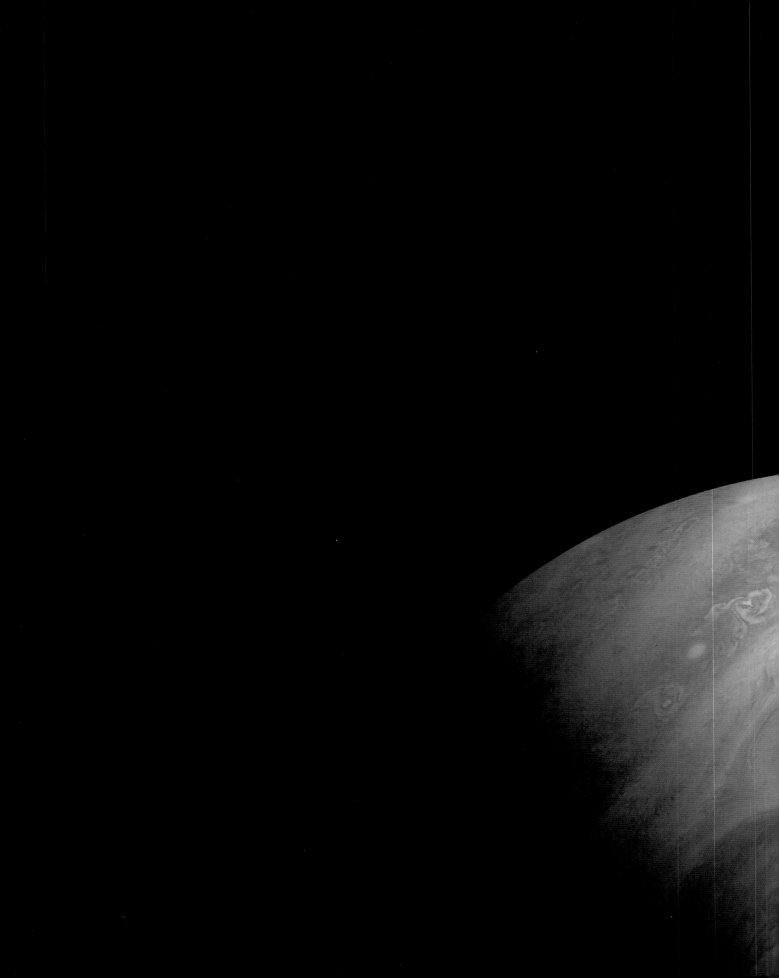

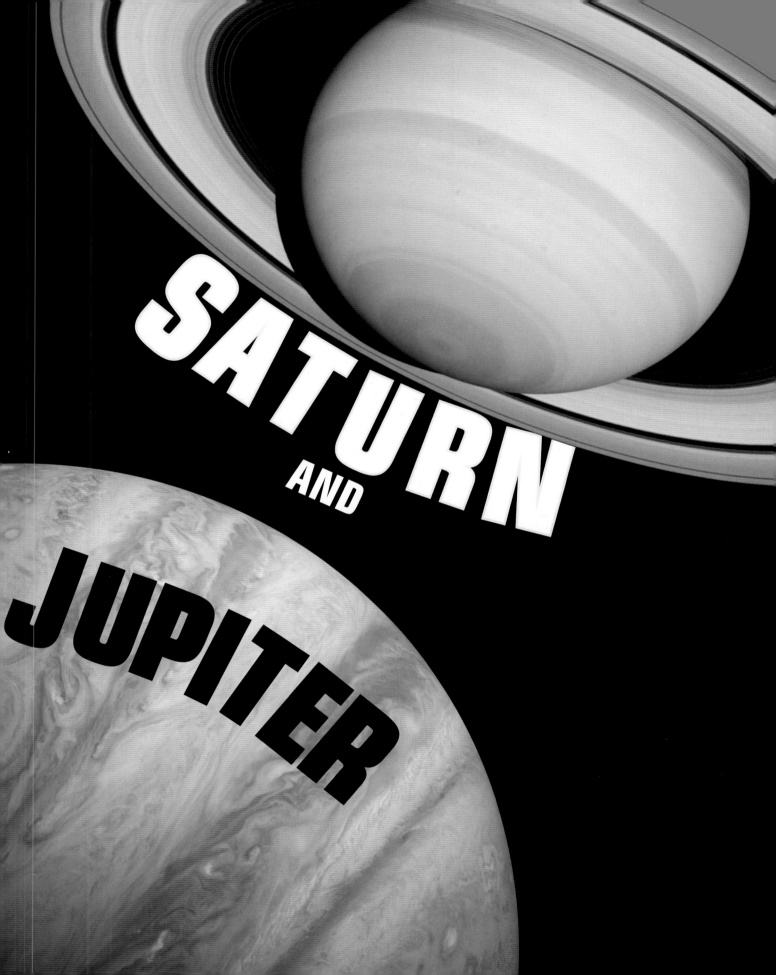

SATURN AND JUPITER

Jupiter

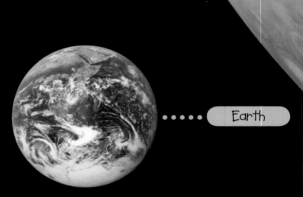

Jupiter is the largest planet in the Solar System.

It is actually bigger than all the other planets put together. Although you could fit 1,321 Earths inside it, Jupiter is still smaller than the Sun. The only solid part of Jupiter is its small, rocky core, or middle. The rest of it is made of gas. All that can be seen are clouds.

Jupiter

Jupiter is the fifth planet from the Sun, between Mars and Saturn. It is a long way from the Sun—five times further from the Sun than Earth.

Earth

For such a large planet, Jupiter spins around quickly. A day on Jupiter only lasts for about ten hours!

STAR FACT!
The ancient Greeks named the planet Zeus after the king of their gods. "Jupiter" is the Roman name for Zeus.

How big is Jupiter?

· · · · · · · · · · · · · ·

Make your own fruit-and-vegetable solar system to show the different sizes (not the shapes) of the planets.

Small bean (Mercury)   Grapefruit (Jupiter)
Grape (Venus)   Orange (Saturn)
Cherry (Earth)   Peach (Uranus)
Pea (Mars)   Plum (Neptune)

Using this scale, the Sun is more than 3 feet across (1 m)—bigger than a hula hoop!

 Jupiter is about 11 times wider than the Earth, but the Sun is 10 times wider than Jupiter!

Jupiter's moons

Jupiter has more than 63 moons.
They are all different sizes, and 14 of them were discovered so recently that they do not yet have names. Four of Jupiter's moons are so big that they can be seen from Earth with a small **telescope**.

Io is the closest main moon to Jupiter. It is very colorful with many **active volcanoes**. Some of the volcanoes are taller than Earth's highest mountain, Mount Everest. The volcanoes produce substance called **sulfur**, making Io yellow in color.

 The volcanoes on Io are hotter than anything else in the Solar System, except for the Sun.

 Io does not have many **craters** because the surface is slowly being covered by **lava**.

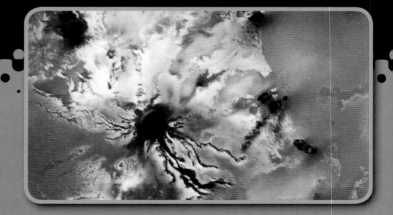

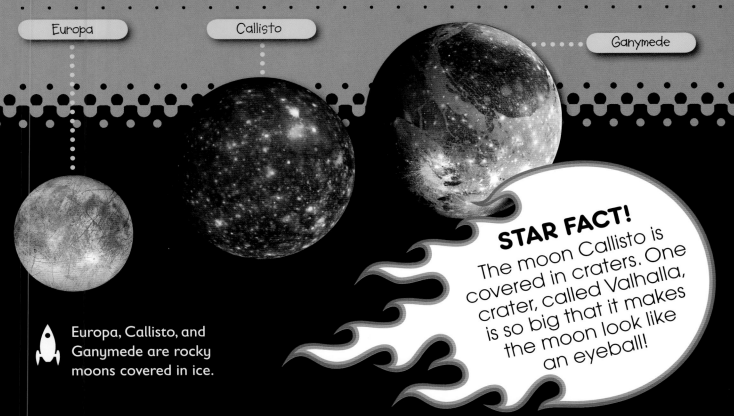

Europa

Callisto

Ganymede

Europa, Callisto, and Ganymede are rocky moons covered in ice.

STAR FACT!
The moon Callisto is covered in craters. One crater, called Valhalla, is so big that it makes the moon look like an eyeball!

Ganymede is the largest Moon in the Solar System. Europa is the smallest of the four main moons. Callisto is in between, about the same size as Mercury. Scientists think that there might be oceans underneath the ice on these moons. A future mission to Jupiter may send a robot to explore Europa.

Galileo Galilei

In 1610, Italian **astronomer** Galileo Galilei discovered Jupiter's four biggest moons—Io, Europa, Ganymede, and Callisto. This is why they are called the Galilean Moons. From 1995 to 2003, the *Galileo* **space probe** orbited, or circled, Jupiter and sent back information about the planet and its moons.

Cloudy planets

Jupiter and Saturn look like giant clouds.

Space probes cannot land on the gas planets because there is nothing to land on.

 On Jupiter, the bright clouds are higher in the **atmosphere** and colder. They are made of crystals of **ammonia**. The dark clouds are lower down in the atmosphere.

Jupiter and Saturn spin very quickly. They both take about 10 hours to spin around once. This fast spinning makes their clouds line up in colored bands, so the planets look striped. It also makes them bulge around the middle.

STAR FACT!
Jupiter seems to be made of things similar to the Sun. It is a bit like a star that never became big enough to start burning.

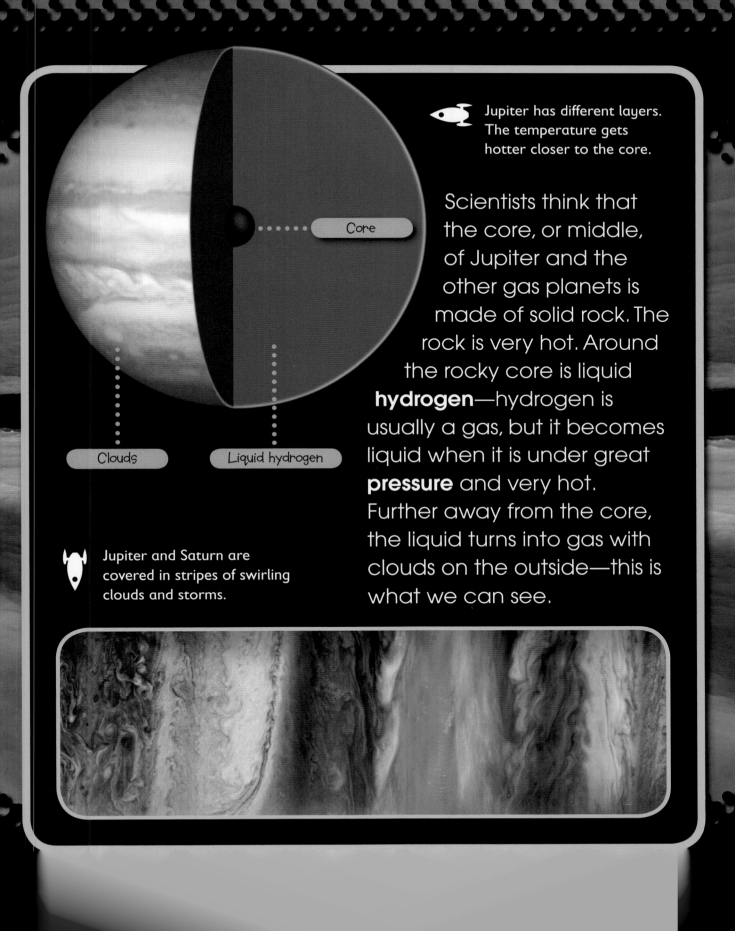

Core

Clouds

Liquid hydrogen

Jupiter has different layers. The temperature gets hotter closer to the core.

Scientists think that the core, or middle, of Jupiter and the other gas planets is made of solid rock. The rock is very hot. Around the rocky core is liquid **hydrogen**—hydrogen is usually a gas, but it becomes liquid when it is under great **pressure** and very hot. Further away from the core, the liquid turns into gas with clouds on the outside—this is what we can see.

Jupiter and Saturn are covered in stripes of swirling clouds and storms.

Stormy weather

Great Red Spot

One of the most incredible things about Jupiter is that it has a large storm called the Great Red Spot.

This giant swirl of red clouds is more than 24,800 miles (39,912 km) across—three times the size of Earth. Scientists have been able to see the Great Red Spot for more than 300 years.

Jupiter and Saturn both have **lightning** storms. These are much bigger than lightning storms on Earth.

STAR FACT!
Temperatures at the top of Jupiter's clouds can drop to -240°F (-151°C). That's much colder than the coldest place on Earth.

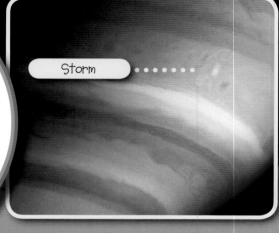

Storm

 The Dragon Storm on Saturn has bright clouds and lightning.

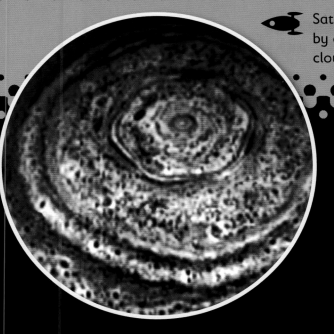

Saturn's north pole is surrounded by clouds with six sides! These clouds are 45 miles (72 km) deep.

Winds on Saturn are six times stronger than the strongest hurricanes on Earth—they can travel at 1,100 miles (1,770 km) per hour!

Saturn has storms, too, but none as big as the Great Red Spot. The strangest storm found on Saturn has six sides, like a honeycomb!

Storm

This is a white, arrowhead-shaped storm on Saturn. The storm is about the size of Earth.

Around and around

Fill a clear cup halfway with water. Stir in different glitter. Swirl the water in the cup. You will see the glitter line up in circles on the surface and in the water. Jupiter's and Saturn's clouds line up like this.

Saturn

Saturn is the sixth planet from the Sun and is also a gas planet with a small, rocky core, or middle.

Saturn is 10 times further from the Sun than Earth. Although Saturn is smaller than Jupiter, it is still massive. It is so big that 763 Earths could fit inside it.

Saturn

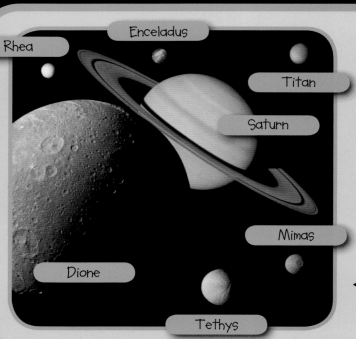

Rhea

Enceladus

Titan

Saturn

Dione

Mimas

Tethys

Saturn has more than 60 moons. Saturn also has rings. They circle around the middle of the planet and were discovered by an astronomer called Christiaan Huygens more than 300 years ago.

 The *Voyager 1* space probe flew by Saturn in **1980** and took pictures of the planet's six main moons.

STAR FACT!
One of Saturn's moons, called Mimas, has a huge crater on one side. When it was hit by a space object, the moon nearly split in two.

Saturn spins very quickly at 2,000 miles per hour (3,219 kph). It spins so fast that Saturn is not actually round like a ball. It becomes bigger around the middle, so seems slightly squashed. It takes about 10.5 hours for Saturn to spin around once.

Rings

Earth

 Saturn is about nine times larger than the Earth and with its rings, it is 21 times wider.

Saturn's rings

Saturn is not the only planet that has rings—all the gas planets have rings. The rings are made from millions of pieces of rock and ice that move around the planet. The pieces are all different sizes—from the size of a grain of sand to the size of a car! The rock and ice in the rings probably came from comets, asteroids, or moons that got too close to the planet and broke up.

As Saturn orbits the Sun, the top, the edge, and then the bottom of the rings can be seen from Earth. This makes the rings look like they are changing shape.

Some of the rings are bright and seem to be full of tiny bits of dust, rock, and ice. Others are dull in color and seem emptier.

The rings are very wide, but thin. They stretch 168,000 miles (270,370 km) across, but are only about 65 feet (20 m)in thickness. If the rings were only as thick as a sheet of paper, they would still be 4,200 feet (1,280 m) across!

Saturn's rings

Cut a doughnut shape out of cardstock and decorate it with glitter. Stick toothpicks around the middle of a grapefruit, and then push the toothpicks through the cardstock. Tilt your model to see how the shimmering rings seem to change shape!

Cassini-Huygens

Saturn

Cassini

Cassini-Huygens **is a space probe that explored Saturn, its rings, and moons.**
A probe is a **spacecraft** that does not carry people. It is sent into space to collect information about a planet or moon.

Cassini-Huygens was launched in 1997. The space probe traveled 2.2 billion miles (3.2 billion km) to reach Saturn. This is more than 9,000 times further than the Moon is from Earth. It took seven years for the probe to get there.

 By the end of 2008, *Cassini* had orbited Saturn 74 times and flown past some of its moons, including Titan.

 Cassini-Huygens was launched into space using a rocket.

Cassini and Huygens

The *Cassini-Huygens* probe is named after two famous astronomers. In 1655, Christiaan Huygens discovered Titan, the first moon around Saturn. In 1675, Giovanni Cassini discovered a gap between Saturn's rings.

Cassini-Huygens was enormous, about the size of a bus. It was actually two space probes in one. *Cassini* orbited Saturn, and *Huygens* landed on Saturn's largest moon, Titan.

STAR FACT!
When *Cassini* arrived at Saturn, it had to fly through a gap in the rings so it could orbit the planet.

The cameras and other science equipment on board *Cassini* helped scientists to find out more about Saturn. Scientists have discovered about 30 new moons and more rings around Saturn. They have even seen fierce lightning storms.

 Huygens was released from *Cassini* by a spring. After 20 days, it went through Titan's atmosphere and floated to the surface using a parachute.

Titan

Saturn's largest moon is called Titan.

It is the only moon in the Solar System with a thick atmosphere and clouds.

The *Cassini-Huygens* space probe arrived at Saturn in 2004. *Huygens* landed on Titan on January 14, 2005. Parachutes were used to slow down the probe before it landed on Titan.

 Once *Huygens* had slowed down enough, it started to send information to *Cassini*.

 Titan is like Venus. Its clouds are so thick that you cannot see through them.

The probe discovered large lakes, rivers, seas, and land. Titan is very cold, so any water freezes. The seas are actually made up of liquid **methane** —methane is normally a gas, but it turns into a liquid when it is very cold.

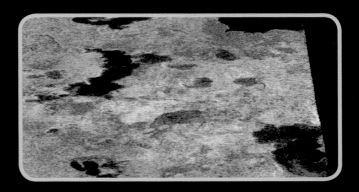

 Cassini found lakes of liquid methane on the surface of Titan.

The space probe also discovered giant dunes, which are like hills, made of tiny pieces of ice and other materials.

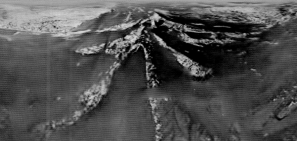

 Huygens took pictures of Titan's surface. These pictures show mountains, valleys, riverbeds, and clouds.

STAR FACT!
Huygens used a parachute that measured 26 feet (7.9 m) across to float down to Titan. It took more than two hours to reach the surface!

URANUS,

NEPTUNE,

AND THE

DWARF PLANETS

Uranus

Uranus is the third largest planet, after Jupiter and Saturn. About four Earths could fit across it. Uranus comes after Saturn, and is the seventh planet from the Sun. It takes 84 years to orbit the Sun.

Uranus is a huge blue-green ball of different gases and it has a core, or middle, of rock and ice. Its surface looks smooth, but it is not solid, so **spacecraft** cannot land on it.

STAR FACT!
On Uranus, winter lasts for 21 years, and half the planet is in darkness. During summer, which also lasts for 21 years, the Sun shines all the time.

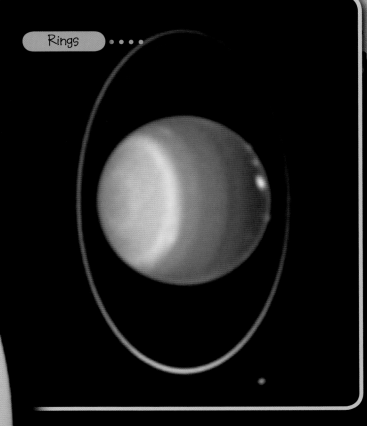

Rings

 Uranus' rings are very faint and difficult to see. Scientists have to use special **telescopes** to see the rings.

The rings of Uranus go from top to bottom. Scientists think that many years ago, Uranus was hit by something very large. It was knocked over and now it spins on its side.

 Uranus is made from gases. A gas called **methane** makes it look blue-green in color.

Discovery

Five planets have been known of for thousands of years because people could see them moving slowly in the sky.

Uranus was the first new planet to be discovered. On March 13, 1781, **astronomer** William Herschel saw something using his telescope that was not on his **star chart**.

Dome

Telescope

 As well as discovering Uranus, Herschel also measured the heights of mountains on Earth's Moon and discovered four of Uranus' moons.

STAR FACT!
Uranus can sometimes be seen from Earth. It looks like a very faint star.

This telescope in Spain is named after William Herschel.

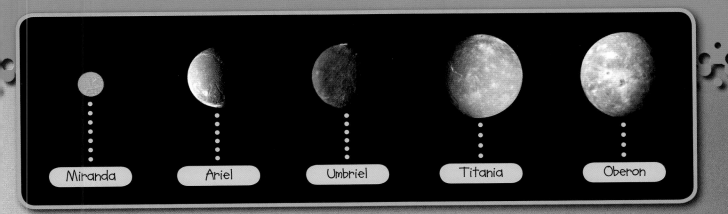

Miranda · Ariel · Umbriel · Titania · Oberon

Astronomers realized that it was a planet, twice as far away from the Sun as Saturn. They also figured out that there should be another planet as well, because Uranus was never quite where they thought it should be. It was being tugged by the gravity of something large. They searched with telescopes and found Neptune in 1846.

 Uranus has at least 27 moons. These are the five main moons. Herschel found Titania and Oberon. Ariel and Umbriel were discovered by William Lassell in 1851. Miranda was not seen until 1948.

 William Herschel's largest telescope took two years to make and was the largest telescope in the world for more than 50 years.

Voyager missions

In 1977, two spacecraft called *Voyager 1* and *Voyager 2* were sent into the solar system.
They both visited Jupiter and Saturn. *Voyager 2* went on to explore Uranus and Neptune.

Voyager 2 took nine years to reach Uranus. It took pictures of the planet and its five main moons. It also discovered 10 new moons. Three years later, *Voyager 2* flew over Neptune's north pole and past Neptune's largest moon, Triton.

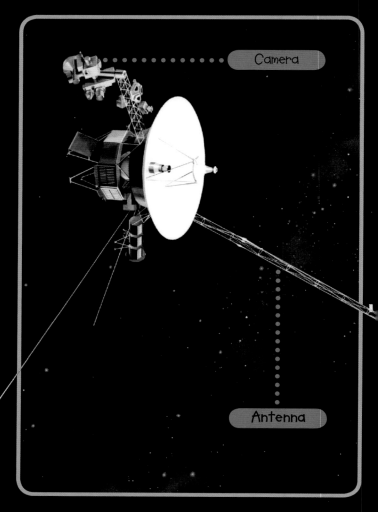

Camera

Antenna

 Voyager 2 has a camera so scientists can find out more information about the planets.

 The south pole of Uranus' Moon Miranda was photographed by *Voyager 2* as it flew by. The moon is only 300 miles (193 km) across.

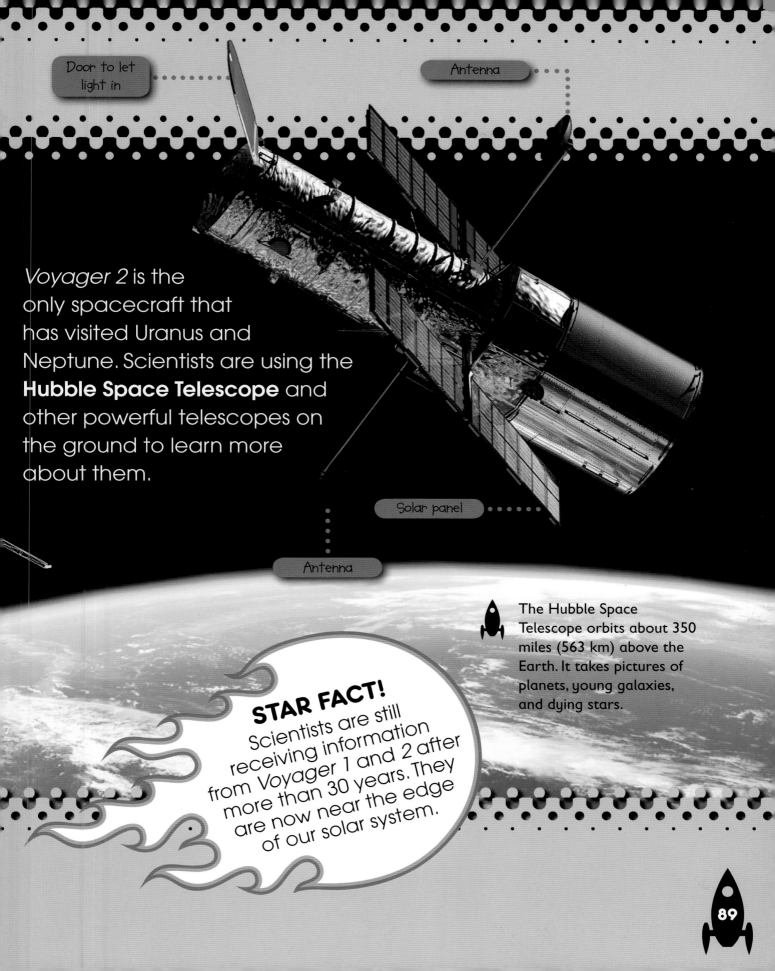

Door to let light in

Antenna

Voyager 2 is the only spacecraft that has visited Uranus and Neptune. Scientists are using the **Hubble Space Telescope** and other powerful telescopes on the ground to learn more about them.

Solar panel

Antenna

The Hubble Space Telescope orbits about 350 miles (563 km) above the Earth. It takes pictures of planets, young galaxies, and dying stars.

STAR FACT!
Scientists are still receiving information from Voyager 1 and 2 after more than 30 years. They are now near the edge of our solar system.

Neptune

Neptune is the farthest planet in our solar system.
Neptune is so far away that it takes 165 years to go around the Sun once. Beyond Neptune, there are only dwarf planets, comets, and asteroids.

Neptune is the fourth largest planet in the solar system. It is slightly smaller than Uranus, and 58 Earths could fit inside it.

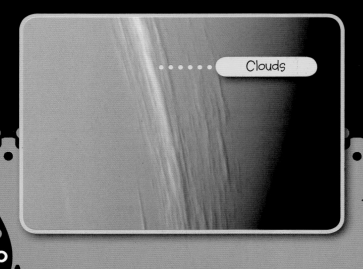

Clouds

Neptune looks mainly blue, but there are some white clouds. These bands of cloud are up to 120 miles (193 km) wide.

Great Dark Spot

 Neptune is made from different gases. One of the gases, called methane, makes the planet blue in color.

Neptune is the windiest planet in the solar system. Winds can reach speeds of more than 1,000 miles per hour (1,609 kph), seven times faster than the strongest storms on Earth. There are huge storms that are about the size of the Earth.

 The Great Dark Spot was discovered by *Voyager 2* in 1989. It has now disappeared.

Where do clouds come from?

Fill a glass with icy water and leave it for 30 minutes. Look at the outside of the glass. What do you see? When warm air hits the cold glass, water droplets in the air turn into liquid water! Clouds are formed in a similar way to this, when warm air hits cold air.

Rings and moons

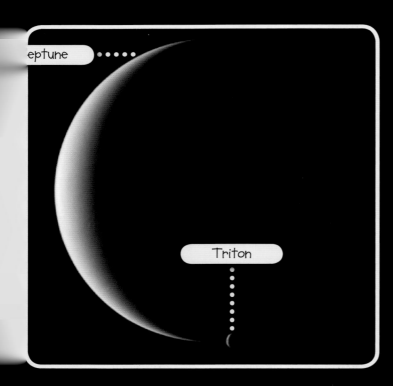

Neptune

Triton

Triton goes around Neptune in the opposite direction to normal moons. It is 1,600 miles (2,575 km) across —a little bigger than Pluto.

Both Uranus and Neptune have rings and lots of moons.
So far, astronomers have found 27 moons orbiting Uranus. Neptune has 13 moons.

Neptune's largest moon is Triton. It was discovered soon after astronomers discovered the planet. Triton is rocky, icy, and very cold, the coldest known object in the solar system. It is red-brown and blue-green in color with pink ice caps.

Ice

Triton is covered in water ice and other frozen gases. Draw a line halfway up a small plastic cup. Fill it with water up to the line. Now freeze the water. What happens to it? Does the water expand?

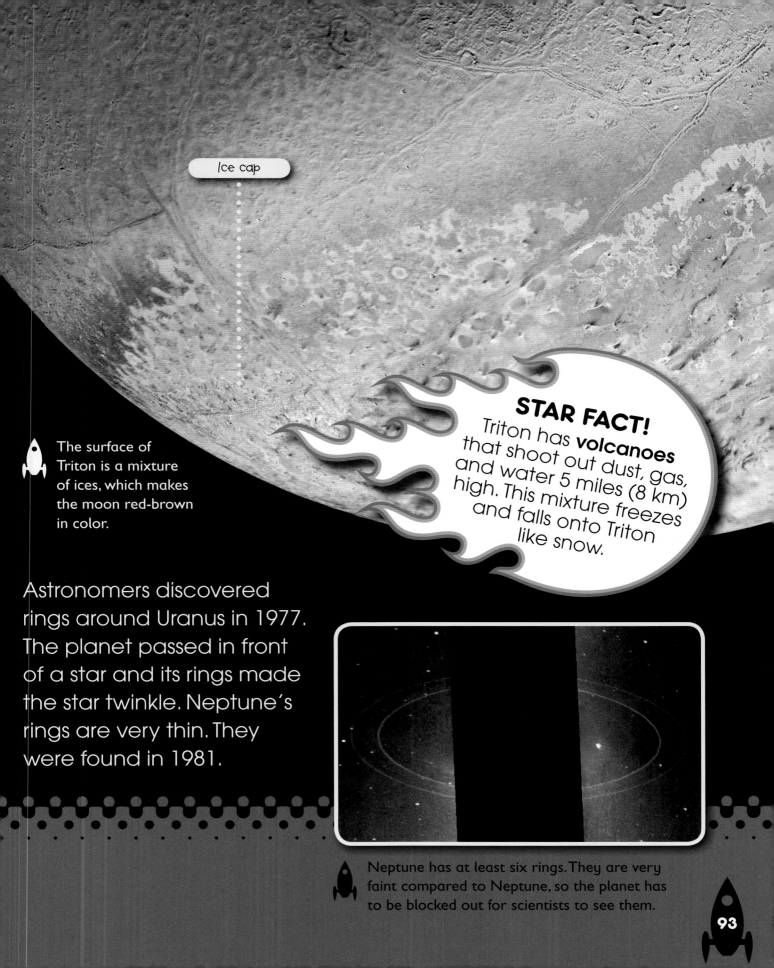

Ice cap

The surface of Triton is a mixture of ices, which makes the moon red-brown in color.

STAR FACT!
Triton has **volcanoes** that shoot out dust, gas, and water 5 miles (8 km) high. This mixture freezes and falls onto Triton like snow.

Astronomers discovered rings around Uranus in 1977. The planet passed in front of a star and its rings made the star twinkle. Neptune's rings are very thin. They were found in 1981.

Neptune has at least six rings. They are very faint compared to Neptune, so the planet has to be blocked out for scientists to see them.

The dwarf planets

Astronomers have recently found more large objects moving around the Sun.
They had to decide if these objects were new planets. Planets are bodies, or objects, that move around the Sun.

Planets are round like a ball. They are big enough to have cleared any rock and ice in their way. These either hit the planet or they were moved out of the way.

Eris and Pluto are farther from the Sun than Neptune. Ceres is in the Asteroid Belt between Mars and Jupiter.

Eris ....

STAR FACT!
Astronomers know of about 100 objects that have orbits like Pluto. They are called the Plutinos and include Orcus, Ixion, Huya, and 2003 AZ84.

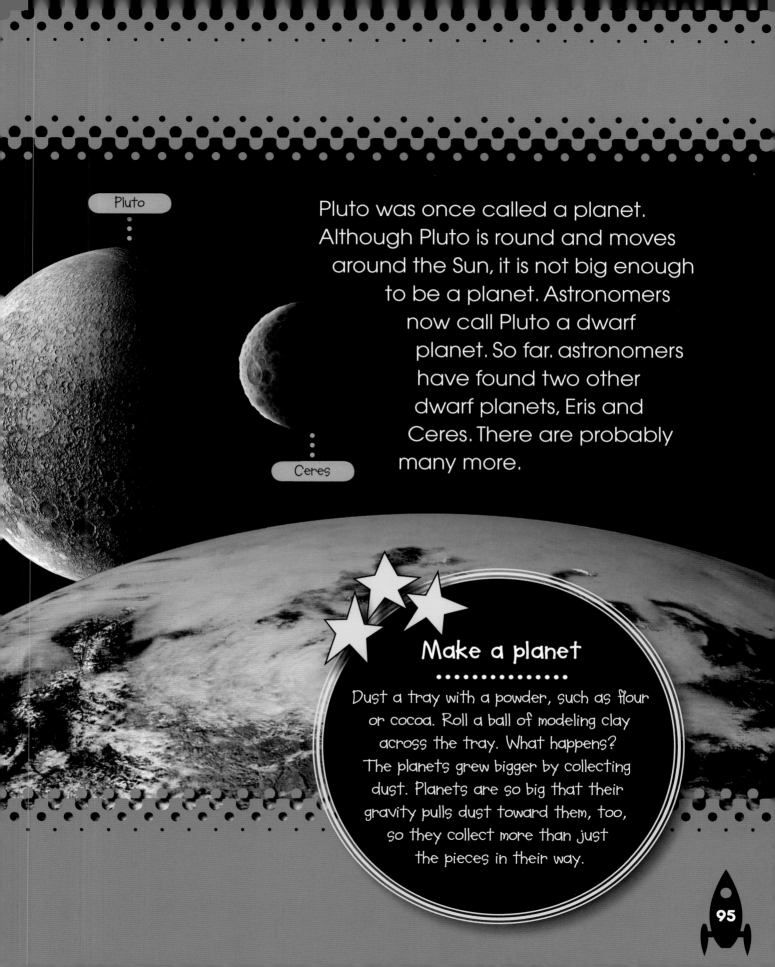

Pluto

Ceres

Pluto was once called a planet. Although Pluto is round and moves around the Sun, it is not big enough to be a planet. Astronomers now call Pluto a dwarf planet. So far, astronomers have found two other dwarf planets, Eris and Ceres. There are probably many more.

Make a planet

Dust a tray with a powder, such as flour or cocoa. Roll a ball of modeling clay across the tray. What happens? The planets grew bigger by collecting dust. Planets are so big that their gravity pulls dust toward them, too, so they collect more than just the pieces in their way.

Pluto

Pluto was discovered in 1930 and was once the ninth planet. However, scientists now say it is a dwarf planet. Pluto is smaller than both the Moon and Neptune's moon, Triton. It is cold and icy, and brown in color.

Pluto has two moons. It also has another dwarf planet near it, called Charon, which was discovered in 1978. Charon is 800 miles (1,287 km) across, which is more than half the size of Pluto. Pluto has two small moons called Hydra and Nix. They were discovered in 2005.

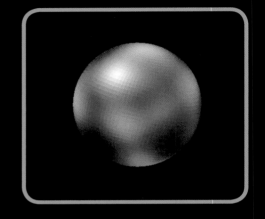

 Pluto is so far away that it just looks gray in color to us.

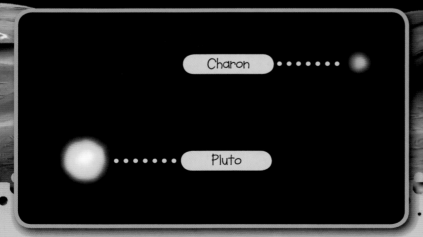

 Pluto and Charon are so far away, they are difficult to see, even with large telescopes.

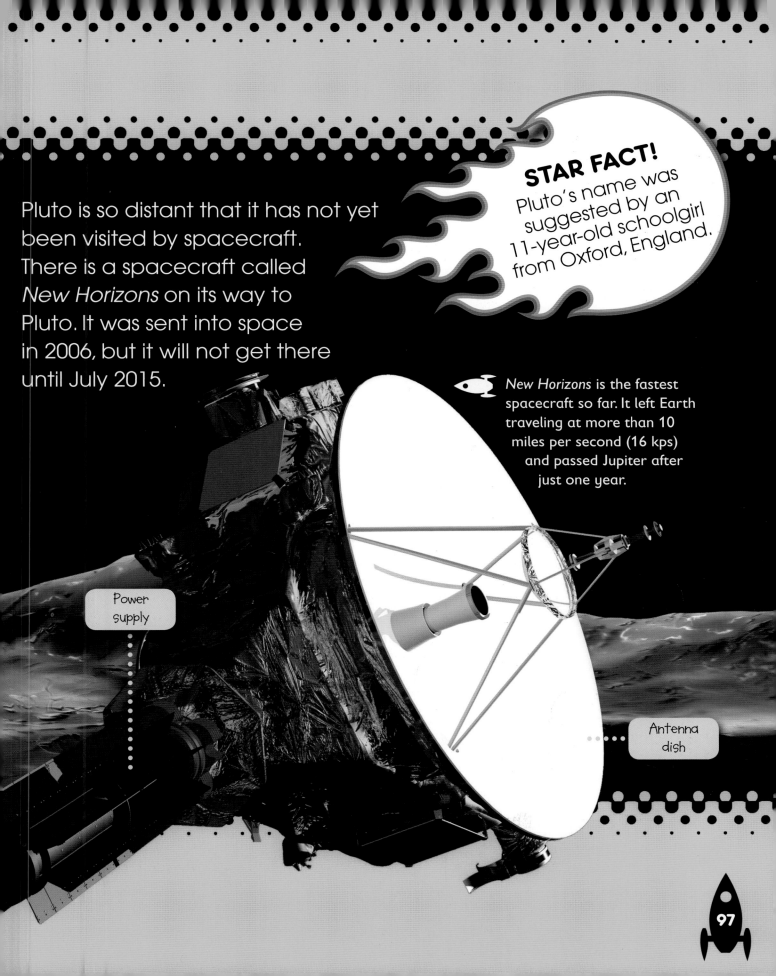

Pluto is so distant that it has not yet been visited by spacecraft. There is a spacecraft called *New Horizons* on its way to Pluto. It was sent into space in 2006, but it will not get there until July 2015.

New Horizons is the fastest spacecraft so far. It left Earth traveling at more than 10 miles per second (16 kps) and passed Jupiter after just one year.

Power supply

Antenna dish

Eris and Ceres

All the dwarf planets are smaller than the Earth's Moon.

Eris is the largest dwarf planet It is slightly larger than Pluto. Ceres is only one-third of the size of Earth's Moon.

 Eris is so far away and faint, even the Hubble Space Telescope cannot see it clearly. Its moon Dysnomia is on the right.

Eris is one of the most distant large objects discovered so far in the solar system. It is a very long way from the Sun—about three times farther than Pluto. It is so far away that it is very faint and was only found in 2003. Eris has a moon called Dysnomia.

 Scientists think that Eris is hard and rocky.

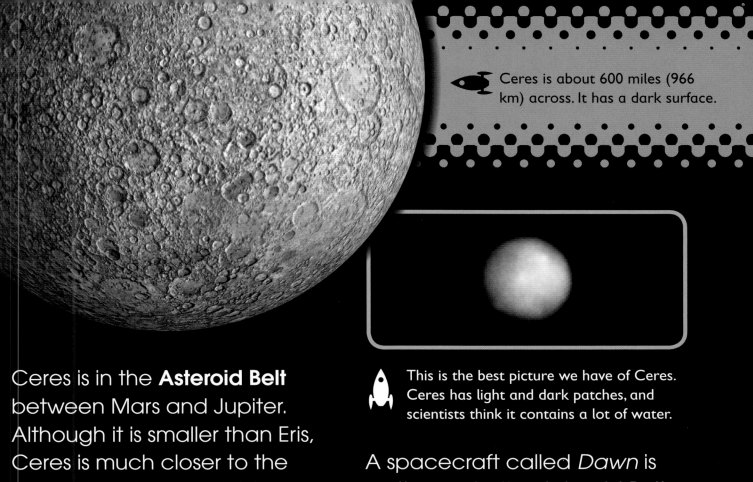

 Ceres is about 600 miles (966 km) across. It has a dark surface.

 This is the best picture we have of Ceres. Ceres has light and dark patches, and scientists think it contains a lot of water.

Ceres is in the **Asteroid Belt** between Mars and Jupiter. Although it is smaller than Eris, Ceres is much closer to the Earth. It is also brighter than Eris, so it was discovered in 1801.

A spacecraft called *Dawn* is on its way to the Asteroid Belt to find out more about Ceres. It was launched in September 2007 and will first go past Mars and then orbit the asteroid Vesta before reaching Ceres in February 2015.

 Dawn will help scientists to find out more about how our solar system was made.

ASTEROIDS, COMETS, AND METEORS

Asteroids

Asteroids are large lumps of icy rock or metal moving around the Sun.

More than 200 years ago, **astronomers** were looking for a new planet when they found the first asteroids. These asteroids are between Mars and Jupiter—in the **Asteroid Belt**.

Gaspra was the first asteroid to be seen close-up by a space probe. It is about 5 miles (8 km) long and 6 miles (9.6 km) wide.

Asteroids often orbit together in groups. Even though there are many of them, they are much farther apart than you might think.

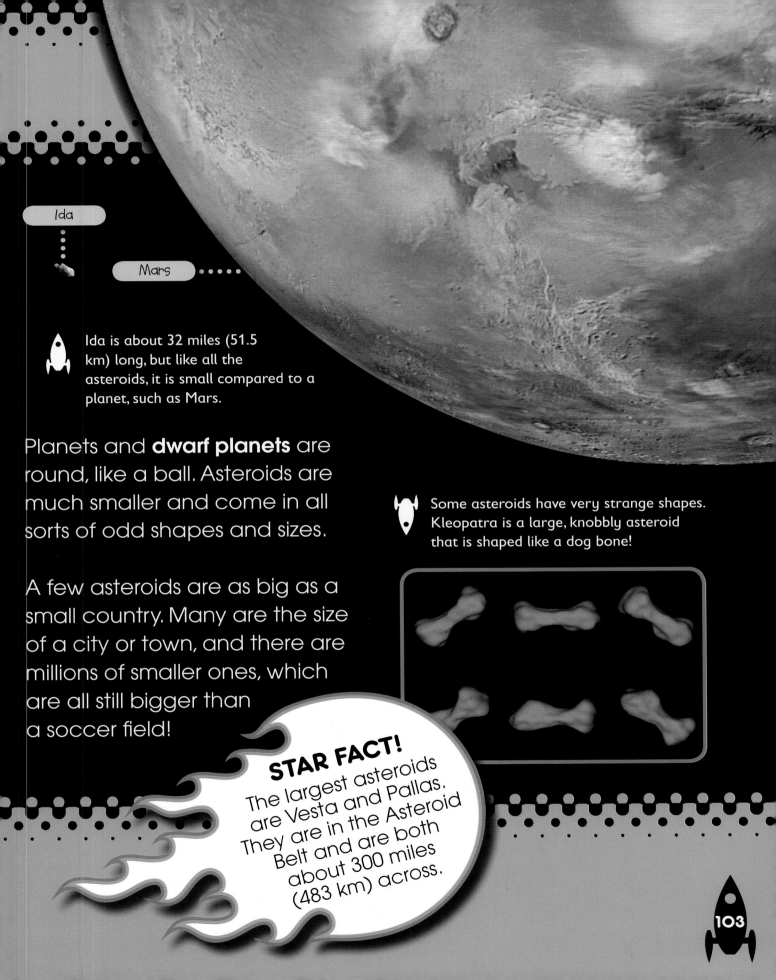

Ida

Mars

Ida is about 32 miles (51.5 km) long, but like all the asteroids, it is small compared to a planet, such as Mars.

Planets and **dwarf planets** are round, like a ball. Asteroids are much smaller and come in all sorts of odd shapes and sizes.

A few asteroids are as big as a small country. Many are the size of a city or town, and there are millions of smaller ones, which are all still bigger than a soccer field!

Some asteroids have very strange shapes. Kleopatra is a large, knobbly asteroid that is shaped like a dog bone!

STAR FACT!
The largest asteroids are Vesta and Pallas. They are in the Asteroid Belt and are both about 300 miles (483 km) across.

The Asteroid Belt

There are lots of asteroids in the solar system and most are found in groups, such as the Asteroid Belt between Mars and Jupiter.

Most of the asteroids in the Solar System are found in the Asteroid Belt. More than one million of them are larger than a mile—as large as 10 soccer fields. There are millions of smaller asteroids, too. The dwarf planet Ceres was the first object found in the Asteroid Belt.

STAR FACT!
If an asteroid gets too close to a planet, it can begin to orbit, or circle, the planet as a moon. Scientists think that the moons of Mars are asteroids from the Asteroid Belt.

Earth

Sun

Mars

Asteroid Belt

Jupiter

 The Asteroid Belt is between Mars and Jupiter. It contains millions of asteroids.

Comets

A comet is like a giant dirty snowball, the size of a town or city.

It is made of ice, dust, and small pieces of rock.

As a comet gets closer to the Sun, it starts to melt. It becomes surrounded by lots of gas and dust. As the comet moves, the dust and gas stretch away from it. This is the comet's tail.

 Gas and dust stream from a comet, creating its tail.

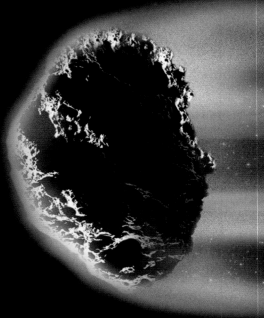

 A comet's tail can stretch for millions of miles across the Solar System.

STAR FACT!
Comets actually have two tails. In the second tail, gas is blown away by wind from the Sun. It is often quite difficult to see.

Sky diary

Ask an adult to help you look into the night sky and keep a journal of what you see. Maybe you will see stars—some might be brighter than others. What shape is the Moon? Can you spot a comet?

From Earth, a comet usually looks like a fuzzy splat in the sky, and it can also have a long tail. You can see comets for a few weeks. As they move slowly across the sky, their tails change length and direction.

Tail

 Comets look fuzzy because they are surrounded by gas and dust. In 2007, Comet Holmes looked like a huge jellyfish in the sky.

Famous comets

Comets often appear reguarly, but the best ones are unexpected.
They grow bright, spectacular tails that can stretch across the sky. After a few weeks, they fade away.

The most famous comet is Halley's Comet. It appears every 75 to 76 years. People have seen this comet for more than 2,000 years. Its orbit takes it out about as far as Pluto.

Great comets

Comet Hale-Bopp

Last seen: 1997

Special features:
It had two clearly visible tails.

 Halley's Comet was last seen in 1986 and it will be back again in 2061.

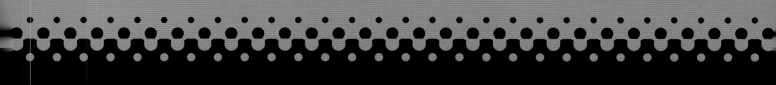

Comet Hyakutake

Last seen: 1996

Special features:
It had an amazing tail.

Comet McNaught

Last seen: 2007

Special features:
It was so bright that you could see it during the day.

Comet West

Last seen: 1976

Special features:
It will not be back for more than 500,000 years.

Edmond Halley (1656–1742)

Halley was an English **scientist**. He thought the comets that were seen in 1531, 1607, and 1682 were very similar and realized that they were the same comet. He believed that it would be seen in 1758—and he was right!

Exploration

To learn more about comets and asteroids, scientists have sent space probes to visit them.
The last time Halley's Comet came close to Earth, the *Giotto* space probe flew close by to see what it looked like. The comet was dark with bright jets of dust and gas.

Halley's Comet

Giotto space probe

 The *Giotto* space probe saw bright jets of gas coming from Halley's dark core, or middle.

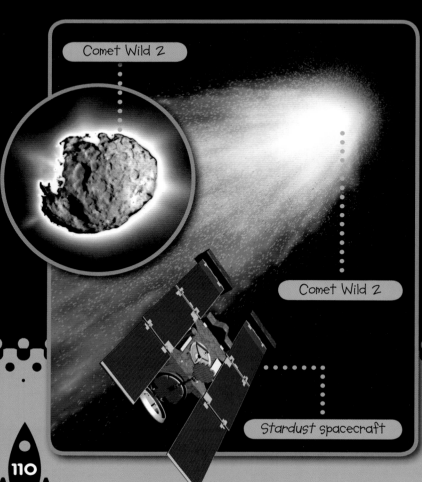

Comet Wild 2

Comet Wild 2

Stardust spacecraft

The *Stardust* **spacecraft** flew through the tail of Comet Wild 2 and collected dust. The dust was brought back to Earth.

The *Stardust* spacecraft has helped scientists to find out what comets are made of.

The *Galileo* space probe was the first to take a close-up picture of an asteroid. It also found an asteroid that has a tiny moon.

Spacecraft have even landed on an asteroid. The Japanese spacecraft *Hayabusa* has collected samples of rock and metal from an asteroid. It will bring it back to Earth in 2010.

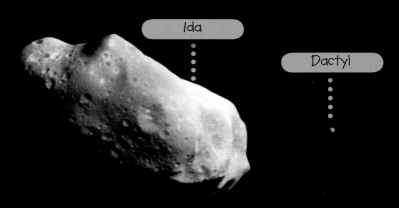

Ida

Dactyl

Ida is an asteroid with its own moon called Dactyl. The moon is about 1 mile (1.6 km) across.

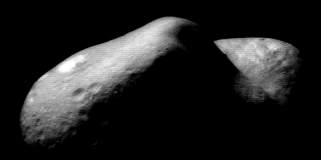

The *NEAR* space probe took many photographs of the Eros asteroid. In 2001, the space probe also landed on its surface.

Stardust

. . . .

Scientists use a gel to catch dust in space. Ask an adult to help you make Jell-O, and use more water than the packet says. Let the Jell-O nearly set and drop in some hard candy. Did they fall to the bottom or stop halfway?

Meteors

As well as large asteroids, there are many smaller pieces of rock, metal, and dust in the solar system, too. These pieces, about the size of grains of sand, are hitting the Earth's **atmosphere** all the time.

 Meteors shoot quickly across the sky. They appear out of nowhere, burn brightly, and then disappear suddenly.

When small pieces of rock and metal hit the atmosphere, they are moving very fast. As they travel through the thick atmosphere, they get very hot and glow. They are called meteors.

STAR FACT!
Some meteors are fast, some are slow. Some are bright, others are dim. Some are colored, and some even explode!

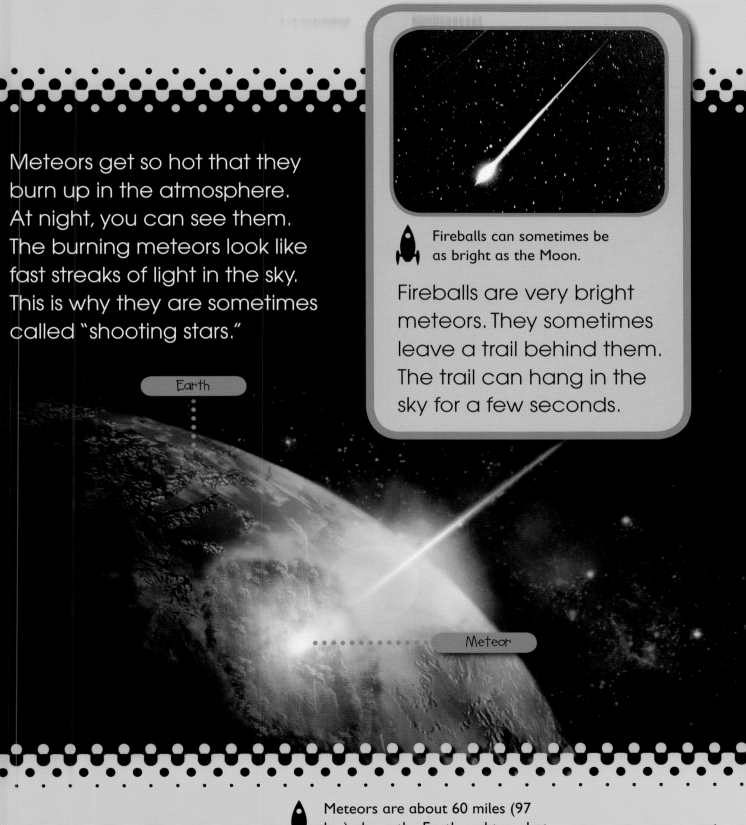

Meteors get so hot that they burn up in the atmosphere. At night, you can see them. The burning meteors look like fast streaks of light in the sky. This is why they are sometimes called "shooting stars."

Earth

Fireballs can sometimes be as bright as the Moon.

Fireballs are very bright meteors. They sometimes leave a trail behind them. The trail can hang in the sky for a few seconds.

Meteor

Meteors are about 60 miles (97 km) above the Earth and travel at up to 40 miles per second (64 kps).

Meteor showers

If the Earth passes through or near the dusty trail left by a comet, we see more meteors than normal. This is called a meteor shower.

Meteor showers occur around the same time every year. As meteor showers come from different comets, each shower is slightly different.

The best showers to see are the Perseids from July 17 to August 24, and the Geminids from December 7 to 13.

STAR FACT!

Meteor showers are named after the star constellation in the sky where the meteors seem to come from.

Looking for meteors

The sky needs to be dark with no Moon, and you need to be away from bright lights. If you can see many stars, you should be able to see meteors. Meteors move quickly across the sky and only a few are bright. Expect to see two or three in 20 minutes.

 In a meteor storm, the meteors are bright and cut across the trails left by stars.

Meteorites

A large meteor might not completely burn up in the Earth's atmosphere.

If it hits the ground, it is called a **meteorite**. There are two types of meteorite—stony and iron.

An iron meteorite was found on the surface of Mars. It was the size of a basketball.

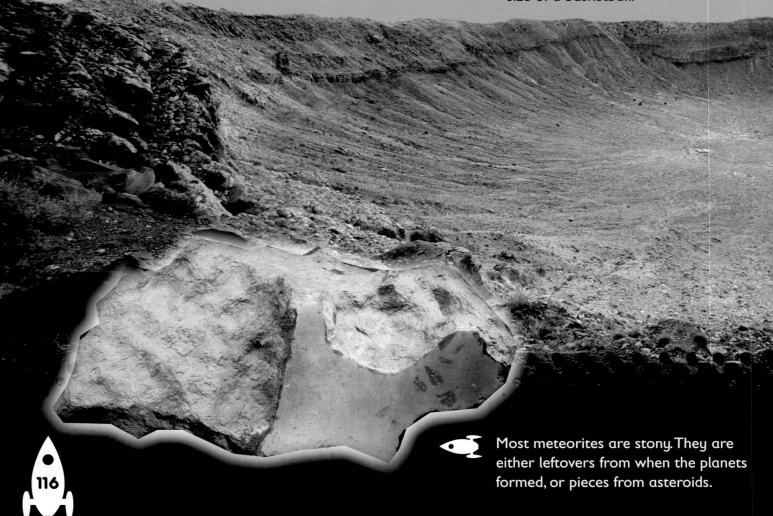

Most meteorites are stony. They are either leftovers from when the planets formed, or pieces from asteroids.

Rocky moons and planets, such as Mars, have lots of **craters**. Craters are the holes left by large meteorites.

The meteorite that made Earth's Meteor Crater was about 160 feet (49 m) across. Astronomers are searching for new asteroids to try to make sure one does not catch us by surprise!

 Meteor Crater, in Arizona, is nearly 1 mile (1.6 km) wide and 600 feet (183 m) deep. Although it is a very large dent in the ground, it is still smaller than craters on the Moon.

STAR FACT!
Scientists think that some meteorites are rocks that were knocked off Mars and have traveled through space before reaching Earth.

Glossary

Active volcano
A volcano—a place where liquid rock called magma comes to the surface—that can still erupt.

Ammonia
A smelly gas.

Antenna
A wire that is used for receiving radio and television signals.

Asteroid
A large lump of rock, too small to be a planet or dwarf planet.

Asteroid Belt
Area between Mars and Jupiter where there are many asteroids.

Astronaut
A person who travels in space.

Astronomer
A scientist who studies the solar system, stars, and galaxies.

Atmosphere
A layer of gases around a planet or moon.

Axis
The straight line through the middle of a planet or moon that it spins around.

Carbon dioxide
Colorless gas needed by plants to grow.

Comet
An object in space made of rock and ice.

Constellation
A named group of stars.

Corona
Hot gas around the Sun.

Crater
A hole made on the surface of a planet or moon by an asteroid or comet.

Dwarf planet
A rocky body that is larger than an asteroid, but too small to be a planet.

Eclipse
When the Moon moves between the Earth and the Sun.

Energy
A source of power, such as electricity.

Gas
A substance, such as air, that is not solid or liquid. Gas cannot usually be seen.

Gravity
Attractive pulling force between any massive objects.

Hubble Space Telescope
A telescope that is orbiting the Earth.

Hydrogen
The lightest gas.

Ice cap
Layer of ice at the north or south pole of a planet or moon.

Inactive (volcano)
A volcano that does not erupt anymore.

International Space Station
Large space laboratory where astronauts can live for months.

Lava
Molten, or liquid, rock that has cooled and turned into a solid.

Lead
A soft, heavy, gray metal.

Lightning
An enormous spark of electricity traveling through the atmosphere.

Magma
Hot, runny rock from the middle of a planet or moon.

Magnet
A piece of metal that can attract iron or steel. It points north and south when held in the air.

Meteor
A glowing trail in the sky left by a small piece of rock from space.

Meteorite
A piece of rock or metal from space that has reached the ground.

Methane
Natural gas.

Orbit
The path of one body around another, such as a planet around the Sun.

Oxygen
Colorless gas needed by plants and animals to breathe.

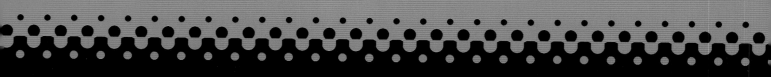

Plain
An area of smooth, flat land.

Pressure
When something is pressed
or squeezed.

Rover
A lunar rover is a car that
astronauts drive on the Moon.

Satellite
A man-made object that orbits
the Earth.

Scientist
A person who studies science.

Solar panel
A panel that changes the Sun's
energy into electricity or heat.

Space probe
A spacecraft without people
on board.

Space shuttle
Spacecraft that has wings to
return to Earth like a glider.

Spacecraft
A vehicle that travels in space.

Star chart
A map of the night sky showing
names and positions of stars.

Sulfur
A solid, yellow chemical.

Telescope
An instrument for looking at
objects that are far away. A
telescope makes the object
appear larger.

Transit
When Mercury or Venus passes
across the face of the Sun.

Volcano
A place where magma comes
to the surface.

Index

Index

Notes for parents and teachers

Sun and Moon

Never look at the Sun directly with your eyes, binoculars, or a telescope. The Sun's rays can damage your eyesight. If you decide to look at the Moon during the day, make sure that your child does not point binoculars at the Sun. This could damage his or her eyesight.

The Sun is much bigger than the Moon. However, if you look at them both in the sky, they seem to be a similar size. This is a perspective effect and happens because the Sun is further away than the Moon. The Moon is 400 times smaller than the Sun, but the Sun is 400 times farther away. The average distance to the Moon is 240,000 miles (386, 243 km). The Sun is 100 million miles (160, 934,400 million km) away.

We can see the Moon because it reflects light from the Sun. It is not a source of light.

Solar eclipses are caused by the Moon moving between the Sun and the Earth. Lunar eclipses are caused by the Earth moving between the Sun and the Moon.

You can experiment with shadows using a flashlight (the Sun) and a ball (the Moon) to mimic the Full and Half Moon shapes and eclipses. Ask someone to shine the light on the ball. Now walk around and look at the ball from different directions. You should see the different phases of the Moon.

Mercury and Venus

Venus can be seen most easily either around sunrise or in the early evening.

Venus stays hot because the atmosphere traps heat from the Sun. You can discuss the common misconception that we get cold because we let cold in. In fact, we get cold because we let heat escape. Talk about which parts of a room are warm and cold.

Heat energy moves by conduction (from object to object—a metal spoon gets hot when it is in a hot drink), convection (when the object itself moves—warm air moving around a room), and radiation (energy transported by waves, such as sunlight).

You can also talk about what materials are best at keeping us warm. Why is a coat better at keeping us warm than a T-shirt? Hot air expands and rises, so it would normally move away from our bodies (convection). Fluffy materials trap the warm air, and keep it from moving away from our body.

Finding ice on Mercury sounds impossible, because it is so close to the Sun. During its long day, Mercury can get much hotter than boiling water. However, some very deep craters near Mercury's north pole are always in shadow. Because Mercury's atmosphere is very thin, it does not help to keep the planet warm.

Observing Mercury is difficult because it is never far from the Sun. The Hubble Space Telescope cannot take pictures of Mercury because it is so close to the Sun.

A day (sunrise to sunrise) on Mercury lasts 176 Earth days. This is twice as long as it takes Mercury to go around the Sun! The planet turns so slowly that when *Mariner 10* flew by, the probe only saw just under half of the surface. The other half was too dark to see.

Earth and Mars

Light travels in straight lines. Shadows are a good way to show this. If light could bend around corners, there would not be any shadows.

Try using a ball and flashlight to simulate day and night. Mark a spot on the ball, and then shine a light on it. As you spin the ball, the spot moves in and out of the light.

Where have the craters gone? The Earth and the Moon are the

same age, but the Moon is covered in craters. Earth has had craters, too, except that most have now been destroyed or hidden. The tectonic plates that make up Earth's surface continually move. This, and the associated volcanism, has destroyed some craters. Wind and water erode the surface, too. Soils and the seas hide others.

Why is Olympus Mons so big? The volcano was made by lava flowing out from under the surface of Mars. The lava stopped flowing a long time ago. This would not happen on Earth, because the top layer of the Earth's surface is moving all the time. As the surface layer moves, it moves the volcano away from the hot spot underneath and a new volcano forms. This is why there are chains of volcanoes on Earth. On Mars, there are no plates, so the volcano stayed in one place and grew larger.

Jupiter and Saturn

Jupiter and Saturn have large magnetic fields, which stretch out into space a long way.

Saturn's and Jupiter's clouds spin around the planets at different speeds, depending on how far they are from the Equator.

Scientists use a parachute to slow down spacecraft where there is an atmosphere, such as on Titan. This does not work on planets, moons, or asteroids without a thick atmosphere. In these cases, scientists use rockets to change the speed of the spacecraft.

You can find out where Saturn is in the sky by looking in a newspaper. It is sometimes possible to see the rings through a very good pair of stabilized binoculars, but to see them clearly, you will need to use a good telescope.

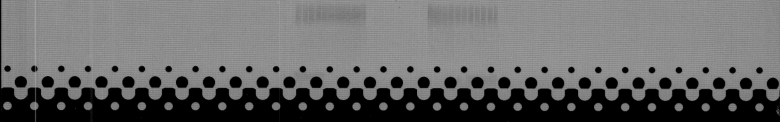

Without a parachute, space probes would fall faster and faster toward the planet or moon that they were visiting. Parachutes cover a large area. The air resistance against the parachute balances against the force of gravity of the falling object, and keeps it from falling faster.

To illustrate how air resistance is related to area, try dropping a flat piece of paper, and see how long it takes to fall to the ground. Now scrunch it up and drop it. It falls to the ground much faster, because it has a smaller area being affected by air resistance.

Uranus and Neptune

What are *Voyager 1* and *2* doing? They have now entered one of the furthest regions of the solar system, where particles from the Sun start to meet those from outer space. They are continuing to make measurements to help scientists understand the outermost parts of the solar system.

Unlike most liquids, water actually expands when it cools and becomes ice. This is why pipes can burst if they freeze and why you should not put full bottles of water in the freezer—as the water expands, it can burst bottles and pipes!

Why does the dwarf planet near Pluto, Charon, seem to stay in the same place in the sky? We see the same side of the Moon because it is rotating at the same rate as its orbit around the Earth. The Earth spins independently so the Moon rises and sets. Pluto and Charon are "locked" together facing each other as they orbit, so from Pluto, Charon seems to hover in the same place in the sky!

The discovery of Eris caused problems for astronomers, particularly when they realized it is larger than Pluto. If Pluto is a planet, then Eris has to be, too. With the likelihood of many more similar bodies, it looked like there would be many more planets.

However, some astronomers had long argued that Pluto was not a "proper" planet, so it was decided to define a new category—the dwarf planet.

Asteroids, Comets, and Meteors

The term asteroid refers to a large rocky body, usually more than 1 mile (1.6 km) across. Some definitions state that an object larger than 160 feet (49 m) across is an asteroid. Bodies that are smaller, such as boulders, rocks, and sand-sized particles, are called meteoroids. Particles that are even smaller are micro-meteoroids and interplanetary dust.

Your eyes get better at seeing in the dark after about 20 minutes. Look halfway up the sky. It is easier on your neck if you can lie down, but make sure you don't get cold.

The most reliable meteor shower is the Perseid shower, which is active from late July through most of August each year, peaking around August 12.

Occasionally, the Earth passes through a very dusty part of a comet's orbit and we see so many meteors that it really does seem like they are raining down. This is a meteor storm. The Leonids, which occur around November 16 to 17, are known for their spectacular storms, but they only occur every 33 years.

The aim of the *Stardust* mission was to capture cometary and interplanetary dust. When the dust met the spacecraft, it was traveling extremely fast—up to six times the speed of a bullet. To slow the particles gradually without damaging them, *Stardust* used a very low density aerogel. This "solid blue smoke" is 99.8 % empty space. The particles embedded themselves in the gel at the end of long visible tracks.